barry joseph weber
david l. downing

object-relations &
self-psychology

a user-friendly primer

University of Indianapolis Press

Planning: Phylis Lan Lin, Executive Director, University of Indianapolis Press
Cover Design and Layout: Edgar Huang
Cover Source: Unknown artist
University of Indianapolis Press Logo: Detail from a painting by Au Ho-nien
Press Editors: Stephanie Seifert Stringham, Peter Noot & Phylis Lan Lin
Press Reviewers: Philip Young & Phylis Lan Lin
Indexer: Marilyn Augst, Prairie Moon Indexing
University of Indianapolis Press Advisory Board (2007–2009):
Mary Moore, David Noble, Peter Noot & Philip Young

Printed in the United States of America

12 11 10 09   10 9 8 7 6 5 4 3 2 1

ISBN: 1-880938-72-0

Published by
University of Indianapolis Press
University of Indianapolis
1400 E. Hanna Avenue
Indianapolis, IN 46227-3697

Fax: (317) 788-3480
E-mail: lin@uindy.edu
http://www.uindy.edu/universitypress

DEDICATION

This book is dedicated to the memory of Barry Joseph Weber, PhD,
25 June 1947–9 March 2002
I also wish to dedicate this book to his children:
Tania Weber Moon
Kate Weber Chiet
Aireal Weber
Barry J Weber II
Finally, this book is dedicated to my children:
Joshua Ladd Downing
Jason Ladd Downing

ACKNOWLEDGMENTS

I t is a difficult task to attempt to summarize and simultaneously do justice to the many individuals and organizations whose support and assistance have gone into the composition and completion of this book. I must begin with an acknowledgment to my late colleague, Dr. Barry J. Weber. Barry approached me many years ago with his idea for a psychoanalytical primer different from any extant text in this well-researched subject area and subsequently asked if I would become the coauthor of the textbook with him—apparently, he appreciated my perspectives and ideas during our subsequent chats. The book was coming together nicely, and we enjoyed our collaboration, which was born of a shared vision of disseminating psychoanalytical thought and clinical practice to successive generations of clinicians—including those who were not interested in undertaking formal psychoanalytical training but were greatly concerned about the effective treatment of often severely disturbed patients. We also shared a vision and a desire to write a text that would be more readily understood than the currently existing texts and perhaps incorporated into programs whose curricula were not necessarily open to psychoanalytical thought. Sadly, Barry was unable to see the project through to completion with me. He died in March of 2002 in his office, having suffered a heart attack at the age of fifty-four while engaged in the moment, doing the work that he so deeply loved.

Assisting us in the beginning as an editor was Ms. Tina Turnbull; her indefatigable efforts, amazing skills, and perspicacity helped us realize the potential of our early labors. This kept us (and, ultimately, me) going. Certainly, I need to weigh in with thanks to the psychoanalysts with whom I have been in treatment, required as part of my training as a psychoanalyst, and those with whom I consulted both before (starting as a teenager in college) and after my formal training. Especial appreciation goes to Ronald E. Fox, PhD, ABPP, past president of the American Psychological Association and founding Dean of the Professional School of Psychology from which I received my doctorate. Dr. Fox, through his good offices, arranged, with Arnold Allen, MD, the psychoanalyst who was then the Chairperson of the Department of Psychiatry, School of Medicine at Wright State University, for me to enroll in all of the Psychiatric Residency Program's psychoanalytical seminars for academic credit, extending across two years of my predoctoral training. This was an extremely gracious opportunity that was quite unheard of and one that enabled me to garner a solid psychoanalytical background while still working on my doctorate with Colonel Robert Reynes, PhD, Moshe Torim, MD, Katherine Dye, MD, and others. This preparation allowed me to enroll later in a course in Cincinnati on Self-Psychology offered by two imminent psychoanalysts in this area of theory and practice: Paul Ornstein, MD, and Anna Ornstein, MD. Especially at that time, this was no small matter for a doctoral student, owing to the restriction of formal psychoanalytical training to physicians except for institutes in the New York City area and (I would later learn) the Center for Psychoanalytic Study in Chicago.

On that note, I wish to thank the faculty and administration of the Center for Psychoanalytic Study for the compelling and rigorous program of training in psychoanalysis that I received during my matriculation, under their mentorship. Special appreciation goes to Lucia Villela-Kracke, PhD, for her support and *strong* encouragement (one could say "kick in the pants") for me to become involved in local, regional, national, and international psychoanalytical organizations and forums. She also encouraged me to write and present on various topics, as did William J. Chestnut, PhD, ABPP of Indiana University, in the arena of short-term psychoanalytic psychotherapy, my first formal presentation to a professional organization—areas in which I was extremely uncomfortable—and has continued to offer her erudite and informed editorial and content insights on my recent papers. Charles E. Turk, MD, continues to be an important sounding board around the arcanum of psychoanalytical theory, practice, and text. He has been a steady voice for more than 21 years in addition to offering an abiding object for identification as he continues to explore new, leading-edge frontiers in psychoanalysis— especially with regard to the treatment of psychosis—and the works of Sigmund Freud and Jacques Lacan, whose works continue to inform my own practice and theoretical musings.

Indeed, Chuck, Lucia, Waud Kracke, PhD, and others who are part of various Chicago-based study groups of which I am or have been a member over the decades, long after any "requirement" necessitated it, have embodied and lived the aspirational call to be "lifelong learners"—and to step outside of the comforts of "the known." Similarly, I am deeply indebted to the principals of GIFRIC (*Groupe Interdisciplinaire Freudien de Recherches et d'Interventions Cliniques et Culturelles*), of Québec: Willy Apollon, PhD; Danielle Bergeron, MD; and Lucie Cantin, PhD, for their collective wisdom and teachings;

their dedication; and the tremendous service to the profession of psychoanalysis, to society, and to the psychotic patients treated through psychoanalysis at their Center, which is called the "388."

I wish to thank James W. Baron, PhD, for enlisting me as part of the contingent that founded the International Federation for Psychoanalytic Education [IFPE], which became such an important part of my emergent identity as a psychoanalyst and psychoanalytic educator and provided me with a remarkable community in which to develop. Through IFPE, I was able to meet and count as colleagues and friends many important people in my life, including Patrick Kavanaugh, PhD; Sue Saperstein, PsyD; Harold Davis, PhD; and many others.

Through Division 39 [Psychoanalysis] of the American Psychological Association, I also have found great encouragement and support from David Ramirez, PhD; Jaine Darwin, PhD; Laurie Bass Wagner, PhD; Mary Beth Cresci, PhD; and Nancy McWilliams, PhD. All of these past or current presidents of Division 39 share a similar vision of ensuring the broadest possible dissemination of psychoanalytical thought, extending this important treatment to underserved and marginalized populations. They also share my passion for creating and maintaining a space for psychoanalysis in the academy. Likewise, I register my appreciation to the membership of the Indiana Society for Psychoanalytic Thought in Indianapolis, especially Elgan Baker, PhD; Stan Osmunson, PhD; and Rick Holigrocki, PhD, for the hospitality and robust psychoanalytical community they opened to me on my arrival in this fair city. The Society's programming is ever-stimulating and has created in Indianapolis a psychoanalytically friendly space.

I wish to thank the Dean of the School of Psychological Sciences at the University of Indianapolis, John McIlvried, PhD, for his support and encouragement regarding this project, for his clear vision of a program of doctoral education in clinical psychology that is inclusive and incorporates the many "camps" to which professionals-in-training should be exposed, *and* for putting a *psychoanalyst* in charge of said graduate programs in psychology. At a time when one is more likely to encounter psychoanalytical theories in programs of gender studies, English literature, film, philosophy, and so forth—but *not* in programs of psychology—John has bucked a decided trend and positioned the program at the University of Indianapolis as a more honestly "generalist" educational program. In this vein, I am most deeply in the debt of Dr. Phylis Lan Lin, the Executive Director of the University of Indianapolis Press, for her belief in this project and her patience with me in completing it in the face of so many professional responsibilities and obligations that leveraged great claims on my time and attention. Dr. Lin introduced me to a wonderful editor, Mrs. Stephanie Stringham. As Stephanie did not come from the field of clinical psychology, let alone psychoanalysis, her trenchant questions and comments were facilitative, greatly assisting me in framing and phrasing the text to do a much better job at what Barry and I had desired—wording arcane and obscure terms and topics in a plain and direct idiom—which is difficult for any psychoanalytical writer, and this one in particular.

I am also indebted to the graduate assistants working with me on various elements of researching the book. Of special note are Michael Jones, MA, and Bryn Higgins, MA, who were instrumental in assisting me in retracing some of my coauthor's steps. Completing the book was encumbered, as I did not have access to my late colleague's notes and archives. Mr. Jones and Ms. Higgins did outstanding scholarly detective work to rediscover research and arcane references that enabled me to reconstruct and elaborate upon Barry's essential ideas where these were left incomplete and to therefore remain as close to his thinking as possible.

I would be remiss if I did not register my deep gratitude to other of my psychoanalytical mentors, especially those who have had some bearing on the preparation of this book. Here, Gerald J Gargiulo, PhD, and Frank Summers, PhD, ABPP, are especially noted. I wish to register my deepest appreciation for the time and consideration given by Christopher Bollas, PhD, perhaps more than anyone on this count, for his considered and thoughtful attention to this book, and for the transmission of his thought and practice through the vehicle of his *Seminars* in Chicago over the past several years, which I was very fortunate to attend. Along with Dr. Bollas, I also must register my deepest gratitude to the late Peter Giovacchini, MD. It was Peter's courage in bucking the hegemonic sway of the traditional, well-entrenched medical psychoanalytical bureaucracy and the received wisdom of the American Ego Psychology paradigm that led him to found the Center for Psychoanalytic Study in Chicago and to catalyze the introduction of U.S. audiences to the works of the British School of Object-Relations and extending psychoanalytical treatment to severely mentally ill patients and others for whom the psychiatric, clinical psychological, and psychoanalytical communities would have turned away as "untreatable" (a trend that a host of mental health "camps" now aim to capitalize on). Thanks must also be expressed to my colleague, Lynne Jansky, DPsa, MSN, for her collaboration in reinstituting the formal operations of the Center for Psychoanalytic Study that we now administer.

I also thank Barry's parents, Linda and Joseph Weber, for their graciousness and steadfast assistance in clearing all of the potential and, most sadly, real and most unfortunate, difficulties in finalizing this project, to make this book a reality. It is my sincere and earnest hope that they are pleased with the results and the last testament to

Barry's life work, which this text, in no small measure, embodies. With the same stroke, I express my most abiding gratitude to my own parents, Bill and Dorothy Downing, for their unshakable belief in the importance of education and the intrinsic value of learning. They, like my grandparents, Fred Downing and Doris Ladd Downing, and my great-grandmother, Berta Barrett Ladd, MD (physician, postmaster, photographer, and all-around trailblazer for her time), always held out the ethos of striving to contribute something to society and of setting oneself to be of service to some greater good. Among the main lessons they have imparted that have lasted a lifetime is the abiding respect for history and what it teaches us. And to my older brother, Nicholas R. Sullivan, who, from a very tender age, taught me important lessons about "ambivalence." I could never have done it without you.

Finally, my deep appreciation to all of the professionals-in-training whose professional development I have been privileged to have been part of over the past 25 years. And to the patients and analysands whom I have treated in psychotherapy and psychoanalysis over the past 32 years, my deepest respect and humble appreciation for entrusting me to accompany them on the most personal of sojourns.

I thank you all for what you have imparted and taught me. Through this book, I endeavor, along with my late colleague, to give something of this largesse back in kind.

David L. Downing, PsyD
January 2009

CONTENTS

FOREWORD

O ver a period of nearly twenty years, we have taught graduate courses in six departments or programs of psychology in the applications of Object-Relations Theories and Self-Psychology to the understanding and treatment of a diverse range of psychopathologies and disturbed mental states. We have reviewed most of the texts, including would-be introductory texts, on the subject. Together, these theories constitute what is described by one author as "the dominant theoretical perspective within psychoanalysis over the last twenty to thirty years."[1] Following such a review, we have arrived at the opinion that, although some of the texts are superior, they actually all have it backwards.

Students do not become interested in Self-Psychology or Object-Relations Theory because of the names of the theorists or because of the longed-for promise of familiarity with and ability to use elaborate and obscure professional terminology and jargon. Rather, they are attracted to Object-Relations Theory and Self-Psychology because these theories are effective in their practical application! Furthermore, psychotherapists find that explanations are provided for *why* they work, even with the most difficult-to-treat patients.

It is only later that psychologists, psychiatrists, clinical social workers, and other psychotherapists become interested in names like Winnicott, Fairbairn, Bollas, Kernberg, Masterson, Mahler, Guntrip, Searles, and Lacan. Novitiates to the practical use of Self-Psychology and Object-Relations Theory then start to become interested in technical jargon they are then able to use and understand—terms such as "splitting," "self-object," "psychotic transference," and "narcissistic extension of the self." Certainly, the frequency with which the terms "Borderline Personality Disorder" and "Narcissistic Personality Disorder" are bandied about these days does provide some attraction. However, for the

---

1   Murray, J. F. (1995). On objects, transference and two-person psychology: A critique of the new seduction theory. *Psychoanalytic Psychology 12*(1), 31–41.

average student or professional-in-training, this interest is quickly abated as soon as he or she attempts to read some of the articles and books on the subject. When one of the authors of this book gave a short lecture on what can kill a theory or put a theory into a coma, one of the students in attendance cogently stated, "Then I can't understand why Object-Relations Theory and Self-Psychology hold on, because they meet all the coma criteria you have mentioned."

The ultimate demise of a theory comes when it fails to make proper predictions or explanations of the things we witness. The flat earth theory died (except for its few humor-loving 21st-century adherents) when ships failed to fall off the edge of the earth. The pure particle theory of light failed to explain diffraction through prisms but later became part of an integrated theory of light, while the "wave" theory of light could explain and predict such diffraction phenomena but not other observable facts about light.

A coma, or something akin to what happened to Sleeping Beauty, can happen long before death. In fact, sometimes the awakening kiss of some new fact or the understanding of an interpreter can bring new life to an old theory. However, theory can be relegated to a sleep as long as Rip Van Winkle's if it does not relate to phenomena that people recognize. It must, then, give those persons the power to "move" the observable events.

One special anesthetic that is even sometimes interpreted as a toxin is, in fact, jargon itself; psychoanalysis and its derivatives have suffered greatly from a profusion and confusion of technical, esoteric jargon. The common reader is often shut out or is confused to the point of futility, while even the experts argue about points that have as much meaning to others as the medieval monks' disputes over the number of angels that could dance on the point of a needle. Both experts and "commoners" are then robbed of the full, robust use of a good theory. Technical language, even jargon, cannot be avoided and is even helpful in some instances as a very precise way of describing something. It is only when the jargon proliferates and dominates the discussion that it puts the audience to sleep.

Our contention *seems* to be the opposite from that of many texts of psychotherapy. Perhaps, like the authors, the reader of this primer may be able to cite a vivid memory, complete with absolute astonishment, as a gifted high school science teacher, or even the host of an educational program on television, first showed him or her what seemed to be an amazing event and then went on to explain it in terms that even we mere mortals could understand. Interest in quarks, particles without mass, and other amazing ideas from higher-energy physics generally does not begin with lectures in college or graduate school; rather, the abiding interest begins with one's own curiosity, born of observations, which then materialize into questions and are followed by the demonstrations of one's teachers.

What far too many texts on psychotherapy seem to do is *assume* that the reader has a *fascination* for the famous characters who came up with some of the original ideas or is looking for technical language that will paralyze debate in any peers. There may be some readers with such bents, but we maintain that the average reader has one question in mind: How do I help the complex person who has come to me for help with their suffering through counseling or psychotherapy? It is our belief that if authors can earn credibility from readers (novitiate psychotherapists) by first helping them with their patients or clients, the novitiate psychotherapist will then be much more likely to seek further gems of knowledge from the original masters or then seek to gather such knowledge in technical concepts. Currently, the average Object-Relations or Self-Psychology textbook seems to be of help to a rather limited crowd, which is most unfortunate, indeed! This is like the sacred books of the Vatican reaching only the best-trained priests or the most advanced books on gastroenterology reaching only physicians specialized (maybe teaching) in that area. Such books have a place, of course, but a theory that works needs a larger readership.

In Objects Relations theory and Self-Psychology we found a whole host of symptomatologies. Some of these are strange psychological phenomena such as hallucinations, unwieldy resistances suddenly appearing and being seen persistently as sinister threats rather than helpers, and even the use of substances to alter mood states. Even more important is that we have found a way to integrate the knowledge into meaningful wholes to be used effectively at the correct time to help persons victimized by their symptoms.

Of course, we do not really mean that we "discovered" these thoughts outright ourselves; each of us stands on the shoulders of quite ordinary people and those of people of extraordinary vision and talents who have sought to help others experiencing psychological distress. In this text, we will try to give credit where credit is due, yet the really exciting thing for us is to find a model of the mind that never seems to leave us feeling flat-footed or without a good idea of what to do when we experience some unexpected human encounter—an occurrence that happens all of the time, by the way.

As good anatomy begins with an understanding of the processes and functioning of the lower species, the theories that are the focus of this book begin with a theory of human development that starts before the "Oedipal" period (that is, at birth). For the faint of heart, however, the innovations described by Object-Relations Theory and Self-Psychology occupy a brief time span (though it can be later fleshed out with many details). Concerned primarily with the first three-and-a-half years of life (the so-called pre-Oedipal period), these innovations can later be integrated with developmental theory covering other periods of life and can be summarized easily. We will endeavor to show how this is done.

It is our hope to counteract the criticisms that we have heard over and over again from professionals-in-training, would-be students of psychoanalysis, and seasoned clinicians, of the literature and techniques of Object-Relations and Self-Psychology. Other teachers in the field also report what we hear repeatedly: namely, that their students find reading about Object-Relations and Self-Psychology to be cumbersome and almost impossible to get through. One of our students mentioned how excited she had been to find a book on the application of Object-Relations Theory to group therapy but how she had become bogged down in jargon and theory and abandoned the book (probably feeling that the book had already abandoned her!) by the early part of the second chapter. Two writers on Kohut's contributions stated that they had repeatedly noticed that the literature on self-psychology was "impenetrable."[2] This is especially so with Kohut, who paradoxically wanted to give his patients usable information that they could "digest" to become "transmuting internalizations." It seems a travesty that the field in which clinicians are supposed to be taught to provide insights that patients can utilize is so unusable to the clinicians who seek to incorporate its knowledge.[3]

Our own experience is that beginners find the literature on Object-Relations Theory no less opaque. There are some excellent books written on both the theory and practice of Self-Psychology and Object-Relations Theory. Almost all of these (if not all), however, are written for experts or persons who are at least intermediately versed in the subject. The present volume attempts to take a different approach, preparing psychotherapists to read these other books, complete with their excellent definitions and fine histories of ideas, by teaching the basic uses of the theories first. Our contention is that the readership of the other books will grow as people gain basic knowledge from a "primer" like this text. Having dealt with "splitting" with the help of at least initial explanations, the psychotherapist will then become hungry for more knowledge on the subject of splitting and on the thought of the psychotherapists of different stripes who have been instrumental in defining the vicissitudes of splitting *for the practical value* such knowledge will have for them in dealing with their patients. (It is hoped that neither Freud nor his followers will object if we use this very fitting term here.)

We are, in fact, so enthralled with these theories and see them as containing answers to dealing with so many short- and long-term patients we see that we have nourished a

---

2   Baker, H. S., & Baker, M. N. (1987). Heinz Kohut's self-psychology: An overview. *The American Journal of Psychiatry*, 144(1), 1–2.

3   See the following classic, which is entirely given over to how persons incorporate experience from others: Shafer, R. (1968). *Aspects of internalization*. New York: International Universities Press. Also see Kohut, H. (1984). *How does analysis cure?* The University of Chicago Press. (See especially pp. 70–71.)

dream of helping to create a "nation of expert psychotherapists." These clinicians will then actually *enjoy* reading books such as *Object-Relations Theory and Self-Psychology: A Comprehensive Text*, by Frank Summers, or even books such as *How Does Analysis Cure?* by Heinz Kohut. We firmly believe that if we start off with explanations and basic applications rather than with the names of the theorists and their jargon, such a revolution will gain a big boost. It is in this spirit that we have written this book.

Also, in the tradition of Loewald, Jacobson, Kernberg, and even Winnicott, the theory and practice described within this book is an integrated theory. No attempt is made to force all people with their problems into difficulties with the pre-Oedipal formation of self-structure so that everyone comes out with some sort of variation of a narcissistic personality disorder or some such. Instead, we attempt to show how these two theories can be embedded sensibly in a larger psychoanalytical-psychodynamic developmental theory that differentiates between the psychotic, the personality disorders, and the less disturbed, with prescriptions on basic treatment strategies for each.

Before concluding, we must make a final disclaimer. Because our endeavor is to introduce and interest people in Object-Relations Theory and Self-Psychology and their applications, our understanding of the theories and their applications may at times seem rudimentary, naïve, debatable, or even reductionistic. Part of that appearance may be our attempt to simplify often-esoteric constructs to make understanding them easier. Another element may be that the authors' own understanding is overly simplistic *in parts* of the theory or history. However, knowing there are so many books already out there authored by theorists and clinicians with greater expertise, we cannot be too upset about this book's possible failing. Our hope is that the following work will draw more readers to books that, until now, only experts in the theories have been reading.

CHAPTER 1

A DIFFERENT STORY AND APPROACH FOR EVERY PERSON

Scenario 1

Joe had barricaded himself in his room by sliding his bed, his dresser, and other items against the door. Inside his room, he was screaming and, by the sound of it, slamming his head against the wall.

The staff was upset and frantic. "Call a code," someone said. "We need some help down here to open that door and restrain him. Get Dr. Smith on the phone and obtain clearance for full leather restraints and Prolixin IM (intramuscular), as well."

Mel, a "psych tech" of some tenure, walked up to Joe's door. "Joe, this is Mel. Talk to me. What's wrong?"

"It's the blood," Joe replied. "Can't you see it coming under the door and across the floor? It's filling my room."

"Joe, I know you don't like Aunt Martha and she is coming here tomorrow, but she's not here now. She comes because she controls all of your money; and I know you think she's not very nice to you, but nothing bad is going to happen. Besides, it's not till tomorrow. She's not here now. Help us open up the room, and I'll come in and talk to you about how we are going to handle her. Yes, I'll be here, and I'll help you handle her."

The head banging stopped. Minutes later, the staff heard some sobbing.

"Joe, are you all right?" Mel asked.

After a pause, Joe replied, "Yes, Mel, my head just hurts."

"Okay, but help me open up the door, and then I'll help you with your head and everything else I mentioned."

A few minutes later, the staff heard furniture screeching across the floor as it was being moved away from the door. Pretty soon, Mel was able to enter, the door closing behind him at first. Soon, he came out. "He's going to need some Tylenol and some bandages. Please let me stay with him, though; it seems to calm him." Mel was allowed to stay, and the crisis faded away like a whimper.

Scenario 2

Sue had been talking almost nonstop for the last 30 minutes. When Dr. Stone even attempted to repeat back empathic paraphrases of what she heard Sue saying, it seemed almost as if Sue treated what Dr. Stone said as little more than interruption. "It is so hard to stay psychologically with Sue," thought Dr. Stone, as she momentarily looked out the window while reflecting on the difficulty.

Suddenly, outbursts came from Sue's mouth: "What are you doing, Betty? I pay you good money to listen to me. I saw you looking out the window. Taking a break, are you? I want that taken off my bill!"

"Sue, I'm sorry. I wasn't really thinking of anyone but you when I looked out of the window. I'm sorry that upset you, though. I guess I was just wishing I could find a way right now to help you escape from the mental trap you feel you are in."

Sue calmed visibly, her eyes searching Dr. Stone's face intensely for signs of sincerity. "Oh, all right, I guess. But you had better be listening to me. I wouldn't be here with you if I didn't need your expert help."

Scenario 3

Josh had missed his three o'clock appointment. There had been no call or explanation. Dr. Brown wondered what had happened. When he called, all he got was Josh's answering machine. That worried Dr. Brown.

At six o'clock, when Dr. Brown went into the waiting room to greet Kristina, who was scheduled to be there, Josh was sitting there, too. "Dr. Brown, can I speak to you for just a minute?" Josh asked.

"Kristina, I'll only be a minute," Dr. Brown stated as he looked at her. She nodded.

Inside the door, Josh started talking immediately; "Dr. Brown, you've got to help me. Elizabeth is moving out."

"Josh, I'm very glad to see you, because I was worried sick when you didn't make your regular three o'clock appointment."

"Oh, yeah, well, I was trying to talk Liz out of moving out. Please tell me how to stop her."

"Well, I want to help you, but I've got to see someone else right now. I really wish you'd come to your appointment; I'm sure that would have helped. I have a nine o'clock cancellation tomorrow morning. Can you make that?"

"Oh, no, that's way too far away. I need advice now. She's packing up right now."

"Josh, like I said, I have a meeting with someone else right now. Would it help if I called you tonight around 8:30? You can hold on till then, can't you?" asked Dr. Brown.

"Oh, Dr. Brown, I don't think I can make it till then. I need help right now. Please!" Josh replied.

"I think you *can* make it. Go home and ask her if she'll talk to you. *Whatever* you do, stay calm and don't get upset, no matter what she does. I'll call, and we'll talk for a few minutes at 8:30 to see how things are going. Then, I'll expect you tomorrow morning."

"I won't know what to say to her. Please, doctor, please."

"Josh, do as I have told you. It *will* be okay, and I'll call at 8:30," said Dr. Brown as he led Josh to the door. "Don't forget to be home and have your answering machine turned off."

Josh left with his head down.

"Kristina?" Dr. Brown called.

......

Later that night, when Dr. Brown called, Josh answered the phone. "Doc, I can't talk much now. It worked just like you said it would. She's still here and talking to me. Right now she's in the bathroom."

"Fine," said Dr. Brown, "Just keep everything on a calm, even keel for tonight and don't forget your nine o'clock appointment tomorrow morning."

"Okay, Doc, I'll be there." Josh sounded much more upbeat as he hung up the phone.

Scenario 4

"Those hands of yours are so red, they are almost rubbed raw," said Dr. Bell with a look of worried concern on her face. "If they get any worse, I'm afraid we're going to have to medicate and bandage them."

Shame filled Frank's face as he looked at the floor.

"Frank, I'm not trying to make you feel worse. I think there must be a reason for all this hand washing."

"I feel like I'm trying to wash off some 'evil' stain that I just can't get off."

"I know this might sound shocking, Frank, but do you think it's possible you might be trying to wash out the wish to put those hands around your father's neck, since he's constantly putting you down and abusing you?" Dr. Bell asked softly.

"I never thought of that before. I don't know; but I love my father," Frank replied.

"Yes, sometimes we love our parents and hate some of the things they do at the same time. I know you'd feel awful if you admitted to yourself that sometimes you'd just like to shut his mouth up, even if it meant choking him."

"I sure am sick of listening to him put me down, but I don't want to hurt him."

"You don't have to choke him in reality. You and I will find a way to stop his terrible attacks on you without physically hurting him. I think, then, you'll find that you won't need to keep washing away a stain that won't go away from your hands."

Scenario 5

Harry had just broken up with his girlfriend and was unable to calm himself. He arrived for his first appointment a half hour early. He was well dressed and gave Dr. Leving a peering, almost hungry, eye contact. During the appointment, he seemed to relax visibly and gave great praise to the few comments that the doctor offered.

At the second session, it was clear that Harry already had been able to use some of the feedback he had received in the first session. He talked about gaining relief because "now I have someone to talk with, almost like a friend." Harry later wondered if "part of the reason I was so absorbed with Gwen was because I had no other friends; I had given up everyone to spend as much time as possible with her."

Soon, it became apparent to Dr. Leving that Harry's father had failed him by his absence during Harry's "formative years" and that Harry's mother had almost used Harry as a substitute spouse. It was clear that Harry needed the kind of same gender rapport, guidance, and reassurance that a close father-son relationship could provide. What amazed Dr. Leving is that Harry was able to take what Dr. Leving had to offer so readily and use what he obtained during the therapeutic sessions to make changes in his thinking, in his feelings, and in his life.

In a relatively short period of time, Harry began making some new friends, and they were people that he could talk with. He also had some conversations with his parents in which he asserted himself for the first time in his life and was able to do so without sounding accusatory. The "load" or pressure on him to get heavily involved with a woman dissipated. Instead, Harry began to devote himself to other interests and to his friends. He showed a great deal of interest in Dr. Leving. Although the doctor did not make a general practice of doing so, he felt comfortable answering Harry's few questions about his background.

Within a few months, Harry seemed back on his feet. He was able to concentrate at work and had no trouble with his sleep. He had met a few women whom he found interesting, but he was in no hurry and seemed to invest almost as much energy in his friendships and in his personal interests.

At their last session, Harry thanked Dr. Leving heartily. "I hope that I can come back sometime if I need a consultation or some 'refueling.'"

"Of course, Harry." Inside, Dr. Leving felt as if he had done very little in this case to help the patient, yet he knew that stating something like that to the patient would not be helpful. Instead, he said, "And Harry, I just want you to know how proud I am of you. You really took hold of your problems and turned them around about as quickly as a person could."

......

How do these psychotherapists know what to do in each case? Are they "master therapists?" If what they do works, *why* does it work, especially when the "cure" is so different in each case?

Alternatively, consider the following two glimpses of sincere attempts to help a person that, in a sense, seem right but just don't work.

Scenario 6

Having recently received his license to practice independently, Dr. Stanford Cline had slowly been building a private practice while he continued his employ at a local hospital. In a few minutes, Dr. Cline would be meeting his eleventh patient, Jack Sanderson, for the first time.

Dr. Cline was thinking with satisfaction over the past few years. He had graduated with distinction, received rave reviews and even a job offer from his postdoctoral site, and had passed the national exam in the top ten percent. Since beginning his own practice some six months ago, Dr. Cline could say that he had not lost a patient unless they had completed work on a short-term problem and were ready for discharge.

Jack had given Dr. Cline no information on the phone. He had sounded guarded and secretive, stating that he would prefer to talk when he got there. Dr. Cline had asked him to arrive a few minutes early to complete registration materials that would be waiting on a clipboard in the waiting room.

When Dr. Cline opened the door to the waiting room, he saw a well-built man in his early thirties sitting by the door. The clipboard was sitting in the chair next to him, obviously indicating that the new patient was done with it.

"Good afternoon, Mr. Sanderson," Dr. Cline said as he walked toward the new patient and leaned over to pick up the clipboard. Out of the corner of his eye, he was sure he had seen Jack flinched as Dr. Cline had moved closer. "Won't you come into the next room with me, where we'll have a little more privacy?" The new patient followed.

After seating himself at his desk, Dr. Cline glanced at the registration materials and found that the forms were all blank. He turned to the new patient, who had again chosen a seat close to the door, almost completely across the room. "Was there some problem with the forms?" Dr. Cline asked gently.

Jack answered gruffly, "I didn't want to write nothin' down."

"Okay, we can complete them later," Dr. Cline said smoothly. He was definitely picking up on some fear and certainly did not want to press the issue right now. "Why don't you tell me what made you decide to give me a call."

At first, Jack's answers were brief. He looked suspiciously at Dr. Cline, who exuded warmth and listened carefully. Dr. Cline was using every ounce of professional acumen to connect empathically with Mr. Sanderson. Soon, words seemed to come easier to the patient.

Jack began by discussing some problems at work. By the time the session was completed, Mr. Sanderson had revealed a host of very difficult problems. Some of the things he mentioned included relationship problems with the opposite sex, same-sex experiences, doubts about his masculinity, descriptions of plotting being done by jealous coworkers, and details of some rather violent physical fights.

As the end of their time together neared, Dr. Cline said, "Well, you certainly have told me a lot, and I'm glad you've come in to see me. I think I can help you." As they rose together, Dr. Cline walked over and extended his hand to the new patient. Jack seemed to take Dr. Cline's hand reluctantly and weakly, even though Jack was obviously a powerful man.

"Everything in here is confidential, right?" Jack asked before leaving. His eyes then seemed to search the room for something, and he said "And there ain't been no tape recordings going on, has there?"

"No, no, of course not. I would never do anything like that without your knowledge and permission. Now, let's make another appointment so we can begin to face some of these problems together, or perhaps you will have further matters you wish to tell me about." They made an appointment for the same time the next week.

The next evening, Dr. Cline received a message on his answering service that a Mr. Sanderson had called to cancel his next appointment. He had left no return phone number and had not indicated whether he wished to reschedule or not. Dr. Cline checked through his records and found the phone number he had originally called when he returned Mr. Sanderson's first call. Dr. Cline made a number of calls at different times during the next few days to no avail, as there was no answer. Finally, on the weekend, when he tried again, he recognized Jack's gruff voice on the other end of the line. "Hello, this is Dr. Cline. I received your message about the cancellation and wondered if the time was inconvenient for you and you wished to reschedule for another time." There was a long pause on the other end.

"How did you get this phone number?" Jack asked, almost with menace in his voice.

"It is the same number you left when you called me the first time," Dr. Cline answered, feeling a rising wave of anxiety. This did not seem to be going right.

"Well, if you know what's good for you, you won't ever call it again." Jack replied.

"Mr. Sanderson, I'm surprised. I thought we had gotten off to a good start. Did something that occurred between us upset you?" Dr. Cline carefully asked, following his training.

"I ain't no sissy wimp, and I won't be talking with a faggot like you. Now, don't ever call me again, or you'll wish you hadn't." With that, Mr. Sanderson slammed down the phone.

Dr. Cline felt a deep fear and upset down to the pit of his stomach. He was also confused. *What* had gone wrong?

Scenario 7

Dr. Cynthia Arness was an experienced clinician who had been working both publicly and privately for eight years. She was waiting for her next appointment to arrive; he was already twenty minutes late, which was unlike him. She thought about Richard: He was charming, but a liar, and regularly on the edge of trouble. She had little trouble understanding him, as he'd grown up deprived, with no father. She felt that they had been making progress over the past several months. Right before Dr. Arness's next appointment, the phone rang. She answered it directly herself, hoping it was Richard. Instead, it was the local police department stating that they had arrested a Richard Rogers for breaking and entering and that he wanted to speak to her. As she had no permission to reveal anything to anybody about Richard, even whether he came to see her or not, she simply remained quiet. In a few seconds, he was on the phone.

"Cindy, I need help, and as you know, I've got nowhere to turn to. They've got me arrested, and I need someone to bail me out."

Dr. Arness squirmed uncomfortably as she thought. She wanted to help; this man had so much potential, and yet, somehow, it seemed like he was asking her to cross a boundary she shouldn't cross. "I don't know, Richard; isn't there anyone else?"

"You know there isn't."

"They have you for breaking and entering?" she asked.

"It was just an accident. I was with the wrong people at the wrong time," he replied.

Deeply troubled, Dr. Arness agreed to come to the station to talk further with Richard later that evening. When she arrived, she could see the skeptical looks on the faces of the officers. "So, do you know his whole record?" one of them asked.

"I think so," she replied, wondering if she did. When she saw Richard, he was all smiles.

"I knew you'd come. Please get me out of here."

"First, tell me what happened," she replied.

"Well, you know how lonely I am and how hard it is for me to make relationships, not having a father and all. I just went for a ride with some guys who ended up in someone else's house. Some neighbor must have seen the lights and called the police. They caught us there." Richard continued smiling in a most charming way.

Before she could reply, a sergeant dropped a computer printout on her table. At the top was someone else's name. About three lines down, under "Also known as," she saw the name Richard Rogers. As she scanned the sheet, she saw a series of charges, mostly having to do with theft, dating back at least ten years. There were also two convictions. "What's this?" she asked Richard as she showed him the front sheet.

"Oh, I guess they keep a record of all the scrapes I ever got in. You see, though, that I was only convicted twice. Both those times, I was a patsy for someone else. I'm sure you understand, since you know how desperate I am for someone to like me." Richard looked very sincere as he talked to her.

"Richard, you never told me about most of this. Here it even says that Richard isn't your real name." The doctor was feeling creepy and desperate herself right now.

Richard hung his head for a few moments and then started crying. "You know how hard it has been for me," he said between sobs.

Dr. Arness was completely at a loss for words. Here, she had attempted to understand and help someone who seemed to be almost a refugee. She'd been supportive and empathic. Now, she found that he'd been deceiving her and, in spite of this, wanted her to bail him out of jail. Finally, she said, "Richard, I need time to think. I won't abandon you, but I can't bail you out. I'll be back to visit you in two days, but you'd better get a lawyer."

Suddenly, Richard's tears dried as he looked up and replied, "I already have one."

Dr. Arness left the station in a hurry that evening. Her head was swimming. She was confused and now knew that she was in over her head. She needed to make a few phone calls and arrange for a consultation with a colleague.

......

The following chapters provide the wherewithal for you, the clinician, to figure out what kind of therapeutic intervention to make with a wide variety of people with varying problems. Certainly, determining the problem (sometimes called finding a diagnosis) is crucial. In addition, having a theory that explains why people do what they do will be helpful. Follow along, and you will soon find that you will also know at least what basic kinds of helpful responses to make to the types of troubled people who will come to you for help. You will also learn what *not* to do, for the same approach does not work with every kind of person or problem.

CHAPTER 2

SINCE BOULDER: A THEORY THAT PRACTITIONERS CAN USE

I n 1949, the fifty-eighth conference of the American Psychological Association (APA) at Boulder, Colorado, settled on a model for psychologists that has guided their training and practice for many years since, although refinements and revisions have been made since then.[4] After reviewing the many years of psychology's history, the Boulder conference formalized the concept that psychology best offered a "scientist-practitioner" model of practice. In a sentence, the theory was that psychology, well-informed as it was through research on human behavior and at the same time increasingly responsible for the relief of human mental suffering, would be served best by an approach that combined the best of both worlds.

Some have called the model a "scientist-artist" model, realizing that psychotherapy is largely an art. Indeed, several conferences of the APA since Boulder (such as at Miami and Vail) and conferences of the National Council of Schools and Programs of Professional Psychology (NCSPP) have attempted to incorporate the artist and scientist ideations, with the concept of "scholar-practitioner."[5] Studies have shown that good practitioners may come from any of a variety of theoretical persuasions and, if they are good, do a number

---

4   See reviews such as Bernstein, B. L. & Kerr, B. (1993). Counseling psychology and the scientist-practitioner model: Implementation and implications. *The Counseling Psychologist, 21*(1), 136–151.; De Piano, F. & Girolamini-Smith, M. (1993). Professional psychology: A model for relevance and effectiveness. *Psychotherapy in Private Practice, 12*(3), 43–52.; and Ellis, H.C. (1992). Graduate education in psychology: Past, present and future. *American Psychologist, 47*(4), 570–576.

5   See a review in Peterson et al. (Eds.). (1992). *The core curriculum in professional psychology.* Washington: American Psychological Association Press.

of things in common, perhaps aided by a psychologist's "sixth sense."[6] At the same time, the burgeoning field of research gave definite direction to psychologists and other mental health professionals about what is best to help a variety of suffering patient types.

More psychotherapists who work from a pure artist-practitioner model made arguments that no theory or model was needed. Good psychotherapy came as much by the "seat of the pants" as it did by anything else, and it was clear that no one theory was superior to others, at least according to current research. Yet others argued that everyone had a theory, whether it be the "if it feels good, do it" theory of the 1960s (which implied that feelings were the central factor in healthy human behavior, to be paid attention to above all else) or a more formally described theory, such as a behavioristic one. Even the "seat of the pants" theory had an underlying belief that psychotherapists' instincts were to be trusted as an almost unerring guide to helping their patients.

Gedo and Goldberg (1973), in their pivotal book, *Models of the Mind*, show how theory and theorists shaped the practice of all psychotherapists. A chief example was Sigmund Freud, whose writings were used to show how his theories and practice changed over the years, conditioned by his training and his experience. Charles Brenner (1973), in his book *An Elementary Textbook of Psychoanalysis*, showed even more thoroughly how Freud's ideas were shaped by his neurological training and by the engineering innovations (such as the use of hydraulics) of his day. Gedo and Goldberg also showed how Freud's ideas changed over the years. In particular, they illustrate a "model of the mind" that Freud used in 1900 (Figure 1) that seems to owe a large debt to hydraulics but contains few terms that people today associate with Freud's work.

Figure 1

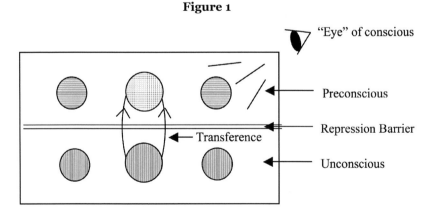

"Eye" of conscious

Preconscious

Transference

Repression Barrier

Unconscious

6   Karasu, T. B. (1986). The specificity versus nonspecificity dilemma: Toward identifying therapeutic change agents. *American Journal of Psychiatry, 143*(6), 687–695.

Gedo and Goldberg also describe and provide a pictorial illustration of what most people conceptualize when they consider Freud's work: his 1923 model, which contains the ego, the superego, and the id (Figure 2).

Figure 2

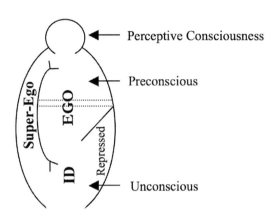

Gedo and Goldberg do not mention that Freud's work underwent yet another major change in the 1930s, with the coming of the Nazis and his increasingly ill health, in which he featured the death drive, or *thanatos*. Which theory of Freud's are we thinking of? It depends on the data he was examining at the time and what therapeutic success he had using the theory.

Some might think of Freud's changing ideas as an embarrassment, but on further reflection, one can see how they fit perfectly with the idea of the scientist-practitioner in that he changed his ideas to fit new information he obtained, whether through clinical experience or other scientifically based information. The rigid clinician is the problem, not the one who updates her ideas, as long as she continues to integrate them into a meaningful system with predictive power that we might call a theory.

A useful example can be obtained in the hypothetical story of the physician Dr. Normal (we will return to his story later in the book), who prescribed penicillin derivatives to all of his patients: Fine, one might think, for those suffering from ear infections or certain other ailments, but what of those afflicted by fractured tibias or some sort of carcinoma? As a secondary prescription for accompanying side effects, a penicillin derivative might be "just what the doctor ordered," but if the patient with the broken leg or cancer left the office with *only* a prescription for Augmentin, the doctor was guilty of malpractice.

What then, about us, the mental health professionals? What if we prescribe psychoanalysis or client-centered empathy for every patient? Are we serving those who come to us for relief any better than Dr. Normal? Maybe too much can be made of the "medical model" in some cases, but we know far too much these days to prescribe and offer the same treatment to someone with a phobia as we might offer someone with obsessional hand washing or someone else with an eating disorder.

The question remains as to *when* we might offer psychoanalytic psychotherapy, Gestalt psychotherapy, Rogerian psychotherapy, behavioral psychotherapy, or whatever. Some practitioners specialize in one sort of psychotherapy and offer nothing else. Even this might be fine, if the doctor recognizes her limits and refers patients with other problems to practitioners whose skills better address the problem. At least psychoanalysts recommend refraining from treating psychotic disorders with traditional psychoanalysis, saying the technique does not work with that population. Other theoretical schools could learn from such appropriate limitations.

We might ask ourselves, "What theory do I use, and when do I use it?" Research in the 1960s indicated that patients improved more than control subjects if the patients were told what kind of treatment they might expect from their clinicians.[7] In those days, most clinicians expected a long process, with free association and many ideas coming from the patient about how to solve his or her problem. With further studies, however, we discovered that the beneficial effect was even stronger if the psychotherapist was told what the patient expected.[8] If the psychotherapists could mold their expectations to those of the patients, at least initially, outcomes were substantially better. The *best* outcomes, however, came when both patient and psychotherapist were educated to one another's expectations so that the match in expectations was good, *with the strongest effect achieved through preparation of the psychotherapists.*[9]

Psychologists are well advised to take the scientist-practitioner method even to the case level, when forming initial hypotheses about their patients to be refined with further data. It is best if this is done consciously, for practitioners must do it anyway.

---

7   See the following studies as examples: Hoehn-Saric, R., Frank, J. D., Imber, S. D., Nash, E. H., Stone, A. R. & Battle, C. C. (1964). Systematic preparation of patients for psychotherapy, I. effects on therapy, behavior and outcome. *Journal of Psychiatric Research, 2,* 267–281.; Sloane, R. B., Cristol, A. H., Perpernik, M. C., and Staples, F. R. (1970). Role preparation and expectation of improvement in psychotherapy. *The Journal of Nervous and Mental Disease, 150,* 18–26.

8   Garfield, S. L. (1971). Research on client variables in psychotherapy. In Bergin, A. E. & Garfield, S. L. (Eds.), *Psychotherapy and Behavior Change* (pp. 191–232). New York: John Wiley and Sons.

9   Jacobs, D., Charles, E., Jacobs, T., Weinstein, H., & Mann, D. (1972). Preparation for treatment of the disadvantaged patient: Effects of disposition and outcome. *American Journal of Orthopsychiatry, 42,* 666–674.

When a psychotherapist encounters a patient, he immediately begins "collecting data" about the other's breath rate, skin pallor, gait, dress, manner of speech, etc. Does the other person look the psychotherapist in the eye? Does she sit comfortably, or is the body stiff and tense? A rigid theory, like "He's a jerk," or a more sophisticated modern version, "He has a narcissistic personality disorder," could wreak havoc on the treatment if the psychotherapist is not open to modifying his ideas with the collection of further data.

This is what science does: it gathers data, forms an initial hypothesis, makes initial predictions, and prescribes initial interventions, all of which are subject to further data collection. In psychological counseling, the scientist-practitioner approach is best used both with patients in counseling and with the study of human nature as a whole. Of course, there is an art as to which of and how these techniques are applied, much the same as physicians are rediscovering the "bedside manner." The physician begins by accurately applying knowledge, like the knowledge out of *Merck's Manual*, which describes the disease, its causes, its sources, and the types of treatment, beginning with the most conservative; that is what is needed in the scientist-practitioner approach.

Modern developmental theory gives us a framework with which to understand general approaches, even if the specific symptomatology requires special considerations. As a mundane example, it is generally accepted that behavioral psychotherapy is more effective in treating children as compared to adults.[10] Psychotherapy researchers are attempting, even today, to codify which treatments are best for which patients and for which problems.[11]

One problem encountered with any theory that even sounds like it follows a medical model is that of apparently useless or even harmful labeling. For a long time, mental health professionals were reluctant to use diagnoses like schizophrenia because the label was likely to stick with the person for the rest of his life (primarily because we seemed to have no really effective methods for ridding the person of the symptoms of the disorder). With the advent of treatment methods that work, including psychoactive medications, the picture has changed. The day is already arriving when one will think it just as ridiculous to label a person a schizophrenic simply because that person had the corresponding symptoms at one time in her life as it would be to label another person a fractured tibia simply because that person at one time had the symptoms associated with that disorder. If diagnosis is like theory, however, in that it is open, postulates causes, and describes a

---

10   Casey, R. J. & Berman, J. S. (1985). The outcome of psychotherapy with children. *Psychological Bulletin, 98,* 388–400.
11   Beutler, L. E. (1991). Have all won and must all have prizes? Revisiting Luborsky, et al.'s verdict. *Journal of Consulting and Clinical Psychology, 59,* 226–232.

course of the disorder and a course of effective treatment, diagnosis becomes not only a friendly, but even a necessary endeavor. This is the true intent of the medical model. If diagnosis fails to do these things, it is not theory building; it does not create a model of the mind and can quickly degenerate into a kind of sophisticated professional name-calling.

In the coming chapters, we invite you to see how good theory leads to correct diagnosis, based on a thorough understanding of aetiology and symptomatology, and how that will lead to prognosis and a series of alternative treatment plans. Specific modifiers may also be present in the form of Axis 1 conditions. Also delineated in the pages of this work is how theory informs the treatment plan. If the treatment plan is observed and followed, based on what is known of developmental theory and what research indicates is the best treatment for each condition, success can almost be assured. In addition, the psychotherapist will know *why* the treatment is working, *when* and *how* to make adjustments, and *what* signifies that progress is occurring. In this sense, mental health can be structured to include the best aspects of the medical model.

Object-Relations Theory offers this framework, and we know of no other mental health theory that can do the same, especially for a wide variety of mental conditions. Even "classical" psychoanalysis, upon which Object-Relations Theory and Self-Psychology are built, and bio-behavioral medicine do not offer the same sort of framework within which to apply so many useful mental health approaches. The theories presented in this book will include directive and managerial, behavioral, relational, psychodynamic, cognitive, and a variety of other therapies. Each of these will be geared to the special needs of certain developmental stages in which needs were not adequately met, so that the "arrest" may be removed and further developmental movement restored or so that a deficit may be filled. The application of these theories will equip patients with the capacities to mature beyond what had been an annoying or painful lifestyle.

As the old saying goes, "The proof of the pudding is in the tasting." We therefore invite you to join us in the coming chapters to explore the usefulness of the claims we have made for Object-Relations Theory and Self-Psychology.

CHAPTER 3

OBJECT-RELATIONS THEORY: PSYCHOANALYSIS AND THE LEGACY OF SIGMUND FREUD

(Magritte's *The Treachery of Images*—i.e., *"Ceci n'est pas une pipe"*)

Exterminate all rational thought—William S. Burroughs

At this point in time, it is difficult to fully appreciate how revolutionary the theories and ideas of Sigmund Freud have been on 20th-century thought (and beyond—so far). Psychoanalysis, certainly one of the greatest intellectual and theoretical movements of our time, has produced monumental changes in our understanding and handling of both normal and disturbed mental states. Part of Freud's greatness was that he devoted himself to some of the more day-to-day aspects of individual life, such as observations about what took place between people or in an individual's thoughts and feelings and how culture could influence a single person. In seeking explanations, he opened the vast and untapped area of inquiry of the individual's internal world or intrapsychic life. For example, Freud was interested in understanding the hidden, "secret" motivations of seemingly purposeful (yet often illogical) behavior, as well as in such "universal" aspects of human existence and experience as dreams, slips of the tongue, and sexuality. We can see this same interest in the works of poets and artists. The Surrealists, for example, had an intense interest in studying and making use of the unconscious and were well aware of how much so-called "reason" actually conceals. The title of Magritte's figurative painting of a pipe, *The Treachery of Images* (which, he helpfully reminds us, is *not* a pipe), contains important implications for psychotherapists of all orientations, psychoanalytical or otherwise. The image, no matter how realistic, is not the same as the pipe itself.

In spite of our culture's widespread use of seemingly Freudian concepts, it is ironic that very few people are actually familiar with Freud's writings. In many colleges and universities, Freud is scarcely mentioned in undergraduate courses of psychology! Even more troubling is the lack of any inclusion of Freud or psychoanalysis in some *graduate* programs of clinical psychology, which are supposed to deal with the basics of development, diagnosis, and treatment of mental illness.

Too often, people associate psychoanalysis, and the person of Freud himself, with a theory and a treatment that became frozen and arrested in time in the first decade of the 20th century. As this chapter will make clear, and the remainder of this primer will make plain, nothing could be further from the truth.*

In fact, as Freud explained, Galileo, Copernicus, Newton, Darwin, Einstein, and he himself (among others) have "disturbed the sleep of the world." All of these people have, at various times, been either idealized or devalued. Each suffered considerable persecution and ridicule within his academic and professional communities. Copernicus suffered great censure after discovering that earth was not the center of our solar system. In the same way, Freud removed the *conscious* person from a position of central control by discovering that *consciousness* is not at the center of an individual's universe. There is something uniquely personal, and therefore imminently more threatening to one's own thoughts, intentions, and behaviors, with Freud's removal of the conscious individual from the center of things. Freud asserted that we are not even the masters of our own *waking* behaviors and intentions, maintaining that many of our actions and motivations exist outside of our conscious awareness and are often best understood by formative early

---

* Psychoanalysis is not only alive, but engaged in a renaissance of clinical and theoretical applications. As a person, and a thinker, Freud continues to be a catalyst for spirited discussion.

emotional experiences of trauma or disruptive patterns in our development. Parts of our past, especially the earliest of our experiences, which occurred before words or thoughts were organized, are incapable of being known to us or remembered even in images, and yet the experience of those first feelings is also incapable of being forgotten. We cannot logically describe in words our perceptual memories of our passage from the womb into the larger world, nor can we describe how we were cared for before we could talk; yet these experiences set basic attitudes of fear, trust, shame, and confidence. Such preverbal images and feelings accumulate during this time and may afterward lead us to group later thoughts and memories with both distorted and accurate associations of our early experiences.

In these and other discoveries, the usefulness of Freud's thought cannot be disputed. Many other theoretical "shifts" or scientific revolutions that have occurred have rarely been the invention of a single individual as, it seems, psychoanalysis is. As diverse as the models of psychoanalysis have become, Freud's writings remain as the guide for all of psychoanalytical inquiry, the practice of psychoanalysts, and the footing for most other dynamic theories of psychology.

People find Freud's writings to be contradictory and inconsistent. They are. However, lest we stop with that as a deadly criticism, remember that the same charge is leveled at both long-enduring theologies and cutting-edge sciences. It is important to note that Freud was a prolific writer; he was an intellectually curious man and a rigorous scientist who, because of new information, periodically revised his previous theories. For example, he was courageous enough to abandon his earlier ideas that all neuroses sprang from the physical action of the nerves and that all neuroses sprang from childhood or infantile molestation by parents.[12]

As Harry Guntrip, a British psychoanalyst and early Object-Relations theorist, observed, "[Freud is] assured of that permanent place in the history of thought that belongs to the genuine pioneer. It is not the function of the pioneer to say the last word but to say the first word. That is the most difficult step. All the pioneer has to begin with is a problem, which has always been there, but hitherto no one has looked at that phenomenon in this particular way. The pioneer suddenly asks a new kind of question."[13]

---

12   It is possible that an individual's true psychological makeup springs from physical action of the nerves or from childhood experiences, but that is not necessarily true for all neuroses. We still see this controversy being played out today with regards to sexuality and childhood abuse, and in recent decades the pendulum has swung away from Freud's earlier theories and toward his later ideas. This shift has reduced the controversy over the accuracy of such "recovered memories" and the so-called "false memory syndrome" that views "recovered memories" as being fantasized (not necessarily in a pejorative or dismissive sense, but with the greatest caution as to the *facts*).

13   Guntrip, H. (1973). *Psychoanalytic theory, therapy, and the self: A basic guide to the human personality in Freud, Erikson, Klein, Sullivan, Fairbairn, Hartmann, Jacobson, & Winnicott.* New York: Basic Books (p. 3).

With this in mind, let us consider another contemporary criticism of Freud and psychoanalysis. Some would maintain that advances in neurology, neurobiology, cognitive-behavioral treatments, and psychopharmacology (to name but a few) have rendered psychoanalysis fit for the ash heap of history; yet even in this era of rampant and uncritical biologism—and its wider expression of blind faith in modern pharmaceuticals—we find recent evidence for the impact of disruptive and ameliorative *experiences*, even through experiments undertaken with the marine snail Aplysia.[14] Kandel demonstrated with his research that environmental influences affect the basic functioning of chemical pathways within the brain; consequently, disturbances of a psychological nature are necessarily reflected in specific brain chemistry changes. Kandel, therefore, asserts that Freud's view that all mental disturbances are fundamentally biological was true. Even more interestingly, the biologically oriented Kandel asserted that implications for psychotherapy were embedded in this set of findings; that is, as experience may modify brain functioning, "it is only insofar as our words produce changes in each other's brains that psychotherapeutic intervention produces changes in patients' minds. From this perspective the biological and psychological approaches are joined."[15]

This leads us to another point: that of the continuing relevance of psychoanalytical theory and all theories that are derived from it. Psychoanalysis is first a theory of personality, emotional functioning, and regulation. Second, it is a method of investigating or researching emotional and mental operations, including even what can go wrong in the development of these operations. Finally, psychoanalysis is a form of treatment for the amelioration of disturbed mental states. We can argue persuasively that the hallmark of any good theory is its capacity to stimulate further thought, inquiry, and scientific investigation.[16] Psychoanalysis has certainly done that. Kuhn has elegantly expressed how theories are developed, mature, and go through subsequent revisions—or even pass out of existence all together. This is similar to the development of a thesis, which produces investigations and a body of evidence that may be both confirming and disconfirming of the original theory: The original theory strives to accommodate this new information and may be more or less successful in doing so, which leads to strains on the original

---

14   Kandel, E. R. (1979). Psychotherapy and single synapses: The impact of psychiatric thought on neuro-biologic research. *New England Journal of Medicine*, 301, 1028–1037. Also: Kandel, E. R. (1983). From metapsychology to molecular biology: Explorations into the nature of anxiety. *American Journal of Psychiatry*. 140, 1277–1293. (Both quoted in Gabbard, G. O. (1994). *Psychodynamic psychiatry and clinical practice: The DSM-IV edition*. Washington, D.C.: American Psychiatric Press Incorporated.)

15   Kandel, E. R. (1979). As cited in Gabbard, G. O. (1994). *Psychodynamic psychiatry and clinical practice: The DSM-IV edition*. Washington, D.C.: American Psychiatric Press Incorporated (p. 16).

16   Kuhn, T. (1962). *The structure of scientific revolutions*. University of Chicago Press.

paradigm as its ideas and concepts become stretched or distorted to take in increasingly discrepant findings.

Eventually, an *anti-thesis* is developed which challenges the prior theory. Out of this dialectical process, a new, emergent *synthesis,* such as Object-Relations Theory, may arise to incorporate aspects of the old antithetical theories into an entirely new theory that may contain elements of both its predecessors. Again, psychoanalysis is far from a "dead language" at this point; indeed, as this book shall make clear, psychoanalysis is by no means any longer a single monolithic theory, method, or set of interventions—and, indeed, it probably never was. Many new "schools" within psychoanalysis have emerged, including two that are prominent on the contemporary scene and that are the subjects of this book: namely, Psychoanalytical Object-Relations Theory and Self-Psychology. These two schools are, in turn, themselves composed of alternative theories, or "voices," and will be explored in this book. Both of these theories, like many others that have evolved from Freud's work, are built on the bedrock of the theory and mode of treatment that calls itself psychoanalytical.

In contrast to classical psychoanalysis and Freudian psychoanalysis, psychoanalytical Object-Relations Theory and Self-Psychology have a greater emphasis on the earliest years of life and the quality of the *relationship* between the mothering-one and the child; there is less emphasis given over to purely biological and genetic factors. These theories also concern themselves with treating more severe kinds of emotional disorders and have extended psychoanalysis and its applications into working with severe personality or character disturbances, even psychoses. Additionally, these theories have a greater emphasis on viewing the *relationship* between patient and psychotherapist as essential to the healing or "curative" aspects of any form of treatment that is undertaken.

Taking into account psychoanalytical theory and the findings of infant-developmental-attachment research, the clinician arrives at an assessment of the nature of a patient's emotional disregulation. Based upon an awareness of the mind (in psychoanalytical terms, the psychic apparatus), the psychotherapist attempts to provide in the treatment relationship a "new edition" of earlier, important relationships (termed "transference") and so offers a new opportunity to evoke, confront, work through, and eventually heal earlier disruptions to the individual's emotional equilibrium. Initially, the patient "hands over" to the psychotherapist certain functions that he or she cannot manage (almost as if the psychotherapist were an auxiliary part of the patient). For example, the capacities for self-soothing, self-calming, and drive regulation may be missing at first and must be performed by the psychotherapist; gradually, healing transformations take place in the treatment, as the patient first receives the regulation of the psychotherapist and then internalizes it, so that he or she is able to manage more and more of these functions autonomously. Traditional psychoanalysts may still believe that healing best occurs by meeting with the patient three to five times per week, in a situation where the patient lies on a couch and the analyst is seated behind; however, a new concept called psychoanalytical psychotherapy, used in particular by those who utilize Self-Psychology and Object-Relations Theory, makes matters such as frequency of scheduling and design of the therapeutic space far less important.

Some Basic Tenets of Freudian Thought

Some of the basic techniques of "classical" psychoanalysis (meeting with the patient three to five times per week, the patient lying on a couch with the analyst seated behind, out of sight) are increasingly questioned, not only by psychoanalytical psychotherapists who may not have undergone full psychoanalysis, but by traditional psychoanalysts themselves. Still, many of the following six basic ideas remain crucial for the actual practice of psychoanalytical psychotherapy by clinicians in their work with any patient. Not all psychoanalytical paradigms or schools of thought necessarily adhere to the majority of these; rather, these tenets constitute the foundations of Freud's own psychology of mind and behavior.[17] Freud approached each patient with whom he worked in very complex ways. He was exquisitely attuned to individual differences and set about finding from each patient as elaborative a history or narrative of the patient's life as he possibly could. At the same time, he was interested in articulating universal laws that governed human mental activity and behavior. The six central tenets that constitute Freud's "Metapsychology" would all need to be addressed in arriving at a proper thorough depiction of any individual and are still very useful today.

The first central tenet of psychoanalytical theory is often referred to as the topographic model. This remains the foundation of anything coming out of the psychoanalytic family. Here, we assert that *unconscious* mental processes exist. For example, Freud noted that patients often couldn't remember many crucial events in their lives but could recall these events under hypnosis. Freud began thinking of the unconscious as divided into two layers (refer to Figure 1 in Chapter 2).

One of the unconscious layers was termed the pre-conscious, which consists of memories or events that could be brought into conscious awareness. Our momentary

---

17   Holzman, P. S. (1970). *Psychoanalysis and psychopathology.* New York: McGraw-Hill.

"forgetting" of something when "put on the spot" is an example of the memory remaining in the system pre-conscious rather than the system conscious, especially when the content is later able to be recalled. The other layer was called the system unconscious proper, whose contents are censored and *repressed* because of their unacceptable or objectionable nature to the conscious mind.

The system Freud designated as consciousness would be considered as resting on the surface of these other systems and is relatively small in capacity. It might be likened to the proverbial tip of the iceberg in relation to the rest of the contents of the psychic apparatus: The unconscious was thought to be infinite in its capacity, in that nothing is ever truly forgotten. The unconscious also was seen as being fairly infantile and as the receptacle for experiences that may have occurred so long ago in the individual's past that there were not even words yet available to name or otherwise describe or locate the experiences. The experiences even may have happened long ago in the history of the species, almost as if the "reptilian" hindbrain could be viewed as a site for the unconscious, while the cerebral cortex might be thought of as a site for consciousness. The unconscious would, therefore, take on very illogical, emotional, animalistic, or even bizarre qualities. The rules of normal conscious logic would not operate here. Ideas would link up with each other in ways such that opposites no longer negated one another, no distinction between past or present existed, and no distinction was seen between wishing something to happen and actually having done something to bring it about in reality.

A second central tenet in psychoanalytical theory is that all behavior is somehow motivated and has meaning; this constitutes the *dynamic* point of view. For example, though the laws of the unconscious may seem absurd or illogical (like the content of our dreams may, at first blush, seem to some), Freud discerned certain processes by which the unconscious is governed and could therefore discern the "meaning" from the so-called madness.

Freud helped debunk the notion that mental illness was somehow a sign of genetic degeneracy or of weakness in the self. He felt that mental health and mental illness ranged along a continuum with all of us governed at some level by our emotional and animalistic roots. Being "normal," especially in the sense of polite society, then becomes a nonsense term unless we consider that all of us are minimally "neurotic" to some degree. We can come to understand various symptoms and behaviors as derived from hidden, unconscious processes that defend us against the embarrassing expression of shameful repressed wishes and feelings. Slips of the tongue, dreams, and even symptoms such as depression and anxiety might be viewed, therefore, as "messages" or "signals" from the region of the repressed unconscious.

Freud also believed in the principle of causality, which is termed "psychic determinism," in which each feeling, thought, behavior, or system is a result of a specific set of intrapsychic causes. It is also the case that the meaning of any one symptom is complex. Indeed, it would be more proper to speak of *meanings*. This notion of multilayered meanings is related to the concept of over-determination, which shows that any single behavior or symptom is the outcome of multiple causes and components of the unconscious. Any symptom complex is a "solution" that may be the expression of conflicting thoughts, feelings, and urges with which the psyche is struggling.

The third central tenet of psychoanalysis is that the past continues to exert an effect on current behavior and emotional functioning. This is termed the *genetic* point of view. As mentioned earlier in this chapter, the origins of psychopathology may reside in very real trauma such as in some form of childhood maltreatment that will leave its mark on the adult personality. It is more often the case, however, that pervasive, yet subtle, trends or patterns that took place during infancy and childhood care and development are similarly central to the development of psychopathology later in life. These may include, among others, long-standing patterns that constituted a lack of attunement in communication with the family, such as growing up in a household that was both excessively critical and lacking in emotional warmth.

We see that "genetic" in a psychoanalytical sense does not refer to our genes or foundation blocks in the biological sense. Instead, it refers to a person's past experiential foundation blocks. Both genetic frames of reference point to the unseen, silent background of the individual's interior that contributes to his or her various behavioral and personality manifestations in the here-and-now. The psychoanalytic "genes" provide a historical context with which to understand and interpret contemporary experience, and thus provide coherent meaning, which leads to healing the conflicts in an individual's life.

The fourth central tenet of psychoanalytical theory somewhat exemplifies the rather pessimistic tone that some critics feel psychoanalysis to be saddled with—namely, that conflict is part and parcel of all behavior. This tenet is termed the *structural* point of view in that it embodies Freud's famous mental "structures" that mediate such conflict: namely the id, the ego, and the superego.[18]

The ego, the id, and the superego should not be construed as some discrete or anthropomorphized set of entities that exist in the brain; rather, these so-called "structures" are most helpfully considered as embodying various functions and capacities of the mind that initiate, govern, organize, or modify emotional and behavioral functions of the individual.

---

18   Freud, S. (1923). *The ego and the id.* New York: W.W. Norton. Also see Figure 2 in Chapter 2.

The unconscious id is the repository of unconscious drives, which Freud hypothesized were basically sexual, survival-oriented, or aggressive in nature. Drives cannot be mentally experienced directly as such, but only through their psychic *derivatives*: ideas, affects, wishes, and impulses. The mental apparatus regulates drives via the primary process (pleasure principle) or the secondary process (reality principle). The id seeks to maximize pleasure, regardless of consequences. The ego operates in such a way as to mediate the pressures for pleasurable discharge of the drives with the demands and needs of the individual in relation to the world-at-large. The drives can be adaptive or nonadaptive, depending on how they are directed. Freud thought that the drives were basically biologically based, arising from within the body and requiring some behavioral response or discharge. Drives can manifest through a variety of means and behaviors. These internal forces (drives) are constant and unrelenting, requiring repeated efforts at discharge; they are seen as the internal motivating sources for all behaviors.

The superego is thought to arise as a consequence of the internalization, on the part of the individual, of the parental prohibitions associated with the Oedipal phase. Throughout one's life, the superego's unconscious reason for being is principally to anticipate the societal regulation of expression of the human, sexual, and aggressive wishes associated with the Oedipus complex. The superego develops by abandoning the extreme black-and-white urges associated with the Oedipal phase. The rules, roles, norms, and mores of culture are passed along in a more stable and modulated fashion: by the individual's identification with the consciences or superegos of the parents. The child internalizes parental and societal values and comes to experience them as his or her own. Other superego functions include approval or disapproval of actions, a critical form of self-observation that utilizes demands for repentance or reparation of wrongdoing, and self-praise or self-love as a result of desirable thoughts or actions.

The ego develops initially as an outgrowth of the growing infant's interactions with its caregivers and with its own body. Indeed, the first ego could be construed as a body ego, according to Freud. This first ego later comes to mediate conflicts between the id and the superego; it represents rational thought, the capacity for delay of impulses, and the various mechanisms of defense against the emergence of unbearable anxiety. Importantly, the ego is the body of *identifications* with objects (people) that have been internalized. Across time, these identifications begin to coalesce into a self, which ranges along a continuum of a (coherent and vital) unity of adaptiveness. The identifications begin as concrete embodiments and mental representations of the infant or child's caregiver(s). Later, these internalized images and object-representations are disconnected from actual people and are "absorbed" into the personality structure of the individual; they are increasingly unconscious aspects of the self. We say: "Well, this is who I am," blissfully unaware of the primary, infantile, and childhood precursors of this "I."

A fifth tenet of the psychoanalytic point of view has been termed the *economic*. This suggests that energy factors within the psychic apparatus produce much of human behavior. The relative strength or weakness of the drives, the ego, superego, and other mediating factors result in behavior or symptoms. We also see this in Freud's controversial notion of libido, which encapsulates the energy quantity of the sexual drive. The degree of the attachment force to any particular object (usually a person) was termed "cathexis."

In terms of the drives, and the sexual drive, in particular, Freud began to speak of "objects," which later became very important in Object-Relations Theory. Freud believed that the sexual drive has a number of component drives, each with its own source, aim, and object. The *source* might relate to the demands of libido associated with any particular developmental period; the *aim* might refer to the discharge of emotion, with an *activity* associated with the discharge. The *object* represents the ultimate "target" of the entire component sexual drive sequence. It is through the object that ultimate drive satisfaction is achieved. As Freud himself noted, the object is usually another person, but if this outlet is prevented, other objects may be substituted. Such substitutive objects, if utilized exclusively, may ultimately lead to the development of a fetish and/or a pervasive, impeding optimal relatedness with other people.

These energic, economic principles concerning the inner workings of the human libido also are seen with regard to concepts such as "fixation" and "regression." That is, parts of the self can become fixated or "stuck" and arrested at earlier developmental stages. Freud hypothesized that these would be the sites of earlier emotional trauma in need of being addressed and worked through in psychotherapy. Such a fixation might often not be seen or evidenced until later in life, at the point of some frustration or similar emotional or physical trauma, which would reactivate that part of the self that is unconsciously lodged in the past. Because of the degree of libido that may be stuck at an earlier stage, there should be a greater chance that the psyche will regress to that area of conflict in the future. According to psychoanalytical theory, the earlier the traumatic event, the more significant a problem it would be for the ego to develop, and the greater the restriction of later emotional growth and development.

In this regard, regression, like any symptom, will serve a number of functions or purposes. For example, regressive processes may represent an attempt to go back to the past, which is still the present at the level of the unconscious, and to "fix" it. For this reason, in a highly symbolic fashion, *all symptoms represent attempts at self-cure and mastery.* This leads us to the final tenet of Freud's overall theory, the *adaptive* point of view. Object-Relations Theory is in accord with the idea that the self is adaptive, since it asserts that the individual strives for contact with the real world via relationships with real people. Even through the use of apparently pathological means, an individual tries to achieve an emotional-behavioral equilibrium and balance in his or her life. Unlike the system unconscious, which operates on the primary process (associated with the id); the system conscious is associated with the adaptive point of view, which stresses the secondary process, or the reality principle (associated with the ego). Secondary process emphasizes adaptation and control, with some culturally accepted gratification of wishes. When functioning via the reality principle, the individual is primarily in the verbal realm, and thoughts are organized in a mostly logical and sequential fashion. The self makes use of external sensory perceptions, attention, and memory—the *autonomous ego functions.* The autonomous ego functions are associated with that aspect of the ego that is, itself, unconscious. The autonomous functions of the ego enable the individual to learn and grow from experience and to modify behavior in accordance with requirements of the external world.

Basic Model of Man

Freud saw man as a producer of meanings, unique in his capacity for self-consciousness, and innately a social being. These thoughts represent something of Freud's Humanistic side. At the heart of the psychoanalytical view of man is a psychological duplicate of the physicist Helmholtz's principle regarding the conservation of energy: Matter and energy can be transformed but not destroyed. For Freud, man was like a hydraulic energy system: Energy flows, gets sidetracked, or becomes dammed up. In all, a limited amount of energy is available, and if it is discharged in one way, there is that much less energy to be discharged through alternate means. The energy employed for cultural purposes diminishes the energy available for sexual purposes, and vice versa. If one channel of expression is blocked, another is utilized, generally along the path of least resistance. This is why the symptoms of an internal conflict are usually not clear-cut, one-to-one expressions; symptoms are far more likely to be disguised expressions of the unconscious drive or infantile "wish" appearing in a dreamlike symbolic manner. Finding the latent, unconscious origins of overt manifestations must be discovered and *reconstructed* through psychoanalytical treatment. Although human behavior may assume a variety of forms, all behavior is reducible to common forms of energy, and the goal of all behavior is "pleasure," which is not hedonism, but the reduction of tension or the release of energy.

Another central tenet of the psychoanalytical model is that man is motivated by two types of drives: sexual and aggressive. Great tension and conflict occur when the expression of the two drives runs into the dictates of society. If human beings simply strove for the immediate and complete gratification of all desires, societal chaos would result. The energy released by individuals must therefore be restricted, inhibited, and channeled if societies and civilizations are to remain stable.

The myriad systems of social relations, culminating in "systems of systems" (societies), are based largely on the renunciation, delay, or redirection of instinctual gratifications. Scientific and artistic endeavors and cultural productivity itself are expressions (sublimations) of sexual and aggressive energy that was prevented from being expressed in a more direct way. Although such transformations of the drives may represent a positive and adaptive outgrowth of the conflict between the instinctual energies of the person and the boundaries created by the requirements of society, other outgrowths for individuals are misery, the forfeiture of happiness, and a heightened sense of guilt (in short, neurosis).

Problems and Psychopathology

Classical psychoanalytical theory asserts that psychopathology is the result of an arrest in development around certain psychosexual stages: oral, anal, and phallic. Symptoms result from the management of instincts, drives, and associated developmental conflicts as they uniquely display themselves in each of the stages.

Freud's idea was that the Oral Stage occurs in the first year of life. Needs, perception, and modes of expression are primarily centered in the mouth, lips, tongue, and other organs related to the oral zone. The Oral Stage is related to incorporating, or taking in. Oral sensations include thirst, hunger, sucking, and satiation. We also know that infants are "hungry" for a variety of stimuli, and *symbolically,* or derivatively, we can equate "seeing," taking things in visually, as part of the Oral Stage. Satiation often follows aggressive behaviors such as the biting, chewing, spitting, and crying that infants display when displeased or in discomfort. Objectives of the Oral Stage include the establishment of a trusting dependence on the mothering-one; there must be optimal provision of gratification of oral libidinal needs in order for this to occur. Severe depressive disorders, dependent personality types, or psychotic disorders are thought to be associated with severe or pervasive lack of satiation in this level of development.

According to Freud, the Anal Stage exists from approximately the beginning of the second year of life until three years of age. The main issue in this stage is the opposition of external control to the basic instincts of the individual child. The arena in which this most likely occurs is with toilet training. When threatened with submission and defeat of the direct expression of instinct, which means a loss of autonomy and self-esteem, the child reacts with obstinacy and defiance. This can result in character traits that could persist throughout life, such as contrary and resistant personalities, as well as indecisive individuals; it is as if the toddler cannot decide how much to "produce" or withhold. Failure to resolve the dynamics of the Anal Stage and associated interpersonal vicissitudes can result in a weakened sense of autonomy, poor self-esteem, lack of initiative, stubbornness, and a tendency toward obsessive-compulsive features.

The Phallic Stage is associated with the period of development between three and six years of age. The child moves increasingly into the sphere of broader interpersonal relationships and begins to operate on a more *social* stage of peer and school-based relationships. From the oneness associated with the Oral Stage and the intense two-person/dyadic relationship of the Anal Stage, the developing child enters into the three-person/triadic relationship of the "Oedipal" phase, which occurs during the Phallic Stage. There is a heightened concern for one's body and its integrity in this stage. Awareness of the differences between male and female anatomy further fuels anxieties about possible castration, loss, incompleteness, defectiveness, and other issues. The child becomes more concerned with who and what he or she is or is not.

In the Phallic Stage, there is a growing awareness of the special relationship that exists between the parents and a sense of being displaced, devalued, and in competition for exclusive possession of the mothering-one. For the boy, this is resolved by surrendering his (incestuous) wishes toward the mother and identifying with (becoming like) the (envied) father, who has what he wants (i.e., the mother). This defensive maneuver to protect a sense of self-esteem and survival is termed *identification with the aggressor.*

The process is more complicated for the young girl. The dominant motivation in becoming interested in the father is the wish to be like the mother and to be loved by or have what the mother has (namely, the father). She wants the father to give her the loving attention that the mother receives. The wish for exclusive possession is ambivalent, however, in that for the first three to four years of her life, she has been attached to the mother and now simultaneously needs and wants to retain this attachment. We see that no such dilemma exists for the young boy in this scenario.

The dominant feature for girls is a turning away from the mother to the father, which will create conflict in her need for attention from the mother. This eventually results in an enhancement of her already established identification with the mother; the ideal resolution being for her to become *like* the person who has her father, so that someday she may possess someone like him. We see these Oedipal struggles in the old saying that men marry someone like their mothers and women marry someone like their fathers: the trite (but also partially true) parody of the "typical" marriage counseling session.

As blockages (fixations) in the optimal development of the individual arise, the intrapsychic world of the individual and the external behavior that expresses that world can become more skewed and rely more heavily upon the maladaptive use or overuse of certain ego defense mechanisms. That's when neurotic symptoms arise. Structurally, the neuroses reflect the conflict between id instincts and the mechanisms of ego defense, neither of which are available to consciousness. In process terms, the neuroses reflect the ways in which the individual attempts to use defense mechanisms to avoid anxiety and guilt (e.g., as administered by the superego) while still allowing for some modicum of control over instinctual gratification.

Symptoms stemming from this stage represent disguised conflicts around sexual and aggressive instincts. Symptoms, and the varied forms they may assume (from the accidental "forgetting" of an important but unwanted meeting to the delusional and hallucinatory psychotic withdrawal from external reality) show the numerous ways in which redirected drives may be manifested as the id impulses strive for discharge. Fixation at or regression to modes of gratification characteristic of an earlier stage of development can be predicted by the nature of the impulses striving for gratification and by the associated defense mechanisms applied to reduce anxiety.

Psychoanalysis is currently enjoying a renewed period of creativity, scientific inquiry, and theory building. Although most Freudian constructs have withstood the test of time and empirical scrutiny, the relative weight assigned to certain constructs might differ, depending on one's orientation within the broad discipline of psychoanalysis. For example, psychoanalytical Self-Psychology (as illustrated in the works of such persons as Heinz Kohut, Ernest Wolf, Arnold Goldberg, Paul Ornstein, and Anna Ornstein) places considerable stress on pre-Oedipal phenomena and the centrality of empathy in working with more primitively organized, and therefore more ill, patients. Likewise, Object-Relations theorists (e.g., Melanie Klein, W. R. D. Fairbairn, Harry Guntrip, D. W. Winnicott, Margaret Mahler) have described a number of developmental phases that incorporate Freud's stages of psycho-sexual and ego development, but with further differentiation, delineation, and emphasis. These psychoanalysts also place additional stress on pre-Oedipal developmental and environmental requirements assumed to be necessary for the optimal development of the individual.

In addition to the centrality of instinctual and intrapsychic forces, psychoanalysts recognize that situational, environmental, and other factors may interact with intrapsychic forces. Such interactions may precipitate the emergence of more undisguised psychological problems. Birth, marriage, death, and other life transitions, either normative or unexpected, can defeat optimal functioning, as they often produce major adjustments within the self and within one's relations to individuals and the world at large.

Straining customary methods of problem solving beyond their typical domain to extraordinary situations can impede effective development and adjustment. A period of disorganization may begin, during which repeated ineffective novel attempts at solution are launched. Given the overall constancy of certain characterological or personality features of an individual, these might be more aptly termed "variations on a theme" as opposed to representing something completely *new*. Eventually, some form of adaptation is achieved that may or may not be in the best interest of the person or his or her significant others (e.g., the psychotic neo-reality, which may include a delusional belief system constructed in the wake of the total inward psychological collapse that accompanies a psychotic break with reality).

The Nature of Change

Bellak and Small (1978) distilled three common stages of all dynamic, psychoanalytically oriented psychotherapy: communication, insight, and working through.[19] These are also essentials of effective treatment. In the first stage, the patient must inform the psychotherapist of his or her problems, history, and current situation; this facilitates the development of a comprehensive, psychoanalytically guided assessment regarding the patient's difficulties, strengths, and deficits.

To facilitate insight in both patient and psychotherapist, Freud stressed the reality of open and honest communication. He developed the fundamental rule of psychoanalysis as one way of ensuring solid communication and overcoming resistances, which the patient typically erects to defend against such open and honest discussion. "Free association" is taken to mean that the patient reports everything that occurs to him or her, no matter how irrelevant, fleeting, trivial, or "crazy" something might appear to be in the light of a

---

19   Bellak, L. & Small, L. (1978). *Emergency psychotherapy and brief psychotherapy* (2nd ed.). New York: Grune & Stratton.

conscious or moralistically based appraisal. Technically, this is the only firm and hard rule of technique in classical psychoanalysis.

Beyond the patient's manifest verbalizations, communication also occurs through what is also *not* talked about (e.g., lacunae, or gaps in the patient's history or narrative). Silences or acts such as facial expressions or body posture also communicate valuable information. Nevertheless, speech is still the prime medium of communication and expression, and it is through speech that the possibility for change occurs in the developing narrative and the relationship that is created with it. This, in turn, carries the possibility for psychotherapy to be successful. In fact, as one senior analyst said to one of the authors, "When a patient *is able* to free associate, the analysis is over."

Even when speech is initially problematic, the analyst should be prepared to wait and at times be silent with the patient; otherwise, there is a risk of impinging on a meaningful process whose ultimate importance and valence cannot be immediately discerned. It may only be much later that the analyst and patient can attach words to ineffable feelings, processes, and experiences. Still, silence may at other times be experienced as a frightening, deadened sort of space. Depending on the quality of this therapeutic space, it may then be more effective for the psychotherapist to be more active, to speak and otherwise assist the patient in getting out of the deadened space, at least for the time being, or until such a time as the patient would have the resources to revisit the deadened space.[20] In this way we can again see how the conduct and process of the psychoanalysis may approximate the individual's own maturation and development from infancy through childhood, adolescence, and adulthood. The psychotherapist, like a good parent, recognizes when it is best to let the patient "bloom" into his own independence and when the patient's dependency prohibits him from doing anything useful, making outside ("parental") help more profitable.

As the patient begins to communicate, the psychotherapist's task is to recognize common themes in behavior, thoughts, feelings, and experiences, particularly as these may relate to the patient's symptomatology. Understanding must include the contemporary patterns as well as the genetic precursors of the patient's current behaviors. Additionally, the nature, quality, and emotional tone of the ongoing treatment relationship must be factored into this configuration. Achieving the type of communication we are describing is a difficult process. An understanding of psychological genetics necessarily contributes to the psychotherapist's understanding of the patient as a unique person, explaining his or her present dynamics and modes of behavior, both adaptive and maladaptive, within the context of his or her life-world.

---

20   Balint, M. (1968). *The basic fault*. Evanston, IL: Northwestern University Press.

In his paper "On Psychotherapy" (1905), Freud spoke of the patient's faith in the treatment he or she seeks. The psychotherapist must recognize and utilize this. Freud clearly saw the principal curative factor in psychoanalysis as the relationship between the patient and the psychoanalyst. He also saw the need for the psychoanalyst to behave prudently and ethically because the relationship can be so powerfully curative. He saw suggestive, directive, instructional, and unduly active therapies as *superimposing* something *onto* the patient that is not the patient's. Psychoanalysis gets at what lies beneath the surface and may be ultimately more real or genuine for the patient.

Any healing psychotherapeutic process is, of course, reliant on the establishment and maintenance of a convivial "working alliance." This involves the willingness of the patient to carry out analytic procedures, identify with and accept the psychotherapist's method of work, and maintain a generally positive attitude toward the treatment. An alliance is an enabling factor that allows the patient to evaluate emotional reactions with a "reasonable, observing, analyzing ego."[21]

The final component of change involves "working through," which consists of the repetition of various interpretations that have been expressed at appropriately timed junctures in the treatment. That is, they are typically delivered, in a hypothetical manner or tone, on the edge of the patient's capacity for apprehending the very same insights for him- or herself. Correct interpretations, however necessary and helpful, are always anxiety-producing. By observing the ground rules for delivery noted above, untoward reactions that may include feelings of shame, emotional injury, or depression can be minimized.

In this way, the patient will be able to receive, understand, and make use of the interpretations; this is essential to firmly establish and thereby confirm the interpretations' validity and accounting for the events that first gave rise to the dynamics being elucidated by the treatment (e.g., identifying common denominators and certain dysfunctional patterns). Because symptoms and personality organizations are fairly robust and resistant to change, these patterns are usually repeated with moderate variations across time.

Freud also emphasized that behavior change occurs through a combination of intellectual and emotional "understanding." Working-through also extends the work of the treatment beyond the limited confines of the patient's relationship to the psychotherapist, enabling the patient to examine the applicability of the treatment to new events and relationships that increasingly have come under consideration in the work of the analysis. The patient's awareness of the unconscious meanings and causes of his or her manifest behavior therefore increases. Essentially, psychoanalysis and psychotherapy are learning

---

21   Bellak & Small, 1978, p. 73.

processes through which the patient's internal personality structure and external behavioral expression of this psychic interior become altered. Through psychological restructuring, therapeutic changes are arrived at via understanding and insight that strengthen the ego. The ventilation of emotion relieves the drive (or its symbolic expressions) or modifies outdated tyrannical superego demands.

When change is not accomplished at this point, it is likely that other causes for the behavior remain unexplained (the symptoms are over-determined). Such gaps in understanding would necessarily blunt the effectiveness, scope of interpretation, and insights within the transference relationship. The therapeutic process would, in such cases, be repeated, clarifying additional determinants of the behaviors and associated symptoms, which, in turn, cycle back into additional working-through. This amounts to additional learning, un-learning, and re-learning.[22]

The Change Process in Psychoanalysis and Psychoanalytical Psychotherapy

In classical models of psychoanalysis, the patient generally lies down on a couch, with the analyst seated behind him or her (out of sight) to create an environment that will facilitate modulated regression, free association, and the maintenance of neutral or projective aspects of the patient's mind. The use of focusing remarks, directing the person's attention to a particular area, or providing additional information so that the interpretations "hang together" or "make sense," is generally effective. Partial interpretations may be given as well, which can lead the person to the major insight that the psychotherapist has discovered or can *test the patient's readiness* to accept the insight. Psychoanalytical theory posits that individuals have at least two motives for entering treatment: to be cured and to *avoid* being cured (discovered, uncovered). As much as patients seek relief from their suffering, the risks, dangers, and psychical pain associated with change are often experienced as being far too great to bear. In other words, a paradoxical reluctance to participate in the treatment process is present from the very outset and must be addressed, at some level, by both the patient and the psychotherapist. A resistant patient becomes "temporarily unwilling or unable to fulfill the terms of the treatment contract,"[23] despite the desire to remain in and benefit from psychotherapy. Psychoanalytical therapists must therefore be attuned to the dynamics of the patient-clinician *relationship* as well as whatever *material* the patient brings to the treatment, in order to differentiate resistance

---

22   Ibid.
23   Weiner, I. (1998). *Principles of psychotherapy* (p.154). New York: Wiley.

from a rational decision to terminate treatment or a reality-based displeasure with the psychotherapist. At any rate, resistance is viewed as a disruption of communication in psychotherapy. The patient ceases to freely communicate salient thoughts and feelings and stops receiving communications from the psychotherapist, blunting the effectiveness of psychotherapeutic interventions.

Resistance is no longer regarded by psychotherapists solely as an obstacle to progress, however. It is now seen as an important subject for interpretation to be explored and understood in its own right, rather than merely being removed or "broken through." Resistance is typically associated with the efforts of a patient to come to grips with interpretations and their implications for the self. Psychotherapy of all types confronts a person with unpleasant or even painful remembrances or sensations regarding him- or herself. Furthermore, it suggests adopting some new and unfamiliar ways of behaving or perceiving. It is not surprising that people wax and wane in their enthusiasm and tolerance for such work. Indeed, those who appear to "coast along" without apparent difficulty in psychotherapy usually lack a meaningful engagement with the psychotherapist or the treatment process.

Reduction or elimination of resistance allows the person to work more comfortably in the psychotherapy, which in turn hastens progress toward fuller self-awareness and behavioral change. In addition to what a patient may learn from content that emerges following the reduction of the resistance, careful considerations of resistant behavior can augment his or her self-understanding (e.g., *Why* has the resistance occurred at *this* particular point? Are there any relationships between resistant behavior seen *in* the treatment and behavior *outside* of psychotherapy?). The patient can achieve an expanded appreciation of his or her coping style, personality makeup, and sources of anxiety.

Finally, interpretation of resistance is often more fruitful than sifting through a mass of undifferentiated and disjointed recollections. This is particularly relevant when one works with the treatment relationship itself, as the relationship is an aspect of interpersonal behavior that occurs in the moment, in the here-and-now of the patient's dealing with the psychoanalyst or psychotherapist. In this regard, such manifestations of resistance can be directly observed and their impact vividly experienced.

Repression and denial are two particularly prominent sources of resistance that traditional psychoanalysts consider. They are also widely involved in symptom formation. Thus, in working more directly with these obstacles to knowledge, the analyst shapes what the patient can gain from the interpretive work of the treatment.

Such interpretation of defenses, which are, at bottom, attempts to *protect* the self from psychological danger, also allows for reduction of psychological suffering; to not further emotionally injure the patient, however, it is often helpful for the analyst to stress how symptoms and defenses have arisen for each individual patient, with full consideration of the developmental context(s) giving rise to each complex.

The Nature of Insight

A discussion of the patient's efforts to *not* know, and to resist the treatment itself, leads us to consider the motive of "insight" itself. Concerning how insight is related to the subjects of defense and resistance, noted above, we are reminded that Freud's early work with Josef Breuer [*Studies in Hysteria* (1895)] emphasizes the workings of "catharsis," which is basically the discharge of dammed-up affect. In his later work, Freud would emphasize the centrality of interpretation, though he stressed that, for treatment to have solid and lasting benefit, change needed to occur in the internal thoughts, feelings, and world of the patient. Insight actually refers to both the intellectual and emotional perception of core themes that have a bearing on the establishment and maintenance of psychological equilibrium. Insight incorporates portions of the self that were previously unconscious into the conscious ego. This, in turn, enhances (1) the patient's and psychoanalyst's total understanding of the patient as he or she functions in his or her contemporary life, in the transference and real relationship to the psychotherapist, and in relation to his or her own history, and (2) especially the patient's understanding and appreciation of the relationship between conscious and unconscious motivations.

Freud realized that making the unconscious conscious was, in and of itself, insufficient to effect lasting behavioral and characterological change (i.e., to break the strength of the repetition compulsion) and lead to cure. The "cure," through insight, involves coming to grips with emotions and wishes that *had* been unconscious and struggling with or reorganizing painful experiences within a relatively safe and benign environment. Psychoanalytic therapy moves the patient first to, and later beyond, fixations associated with earlier stages of development. Insight includes the perception by the patient of conflicts that have been inadequately resolved. This, in turn, reduces the need for repression and thus provides a second chance for the patient to achieve a solution to long-standing emotional problems. As conflicts, needs, wishes, and the associated prohibitions against the wish emerge in the treatment, the patient *and* the psychotherapist are able to gain insight into the instinctual and defensive components of the original conflicts. This understanding is meaningful because of the emotional investment in the situation and in the person of the psychoanalyst, who is part of the therapeutic surround. Change occurs when the patient realizes, on both an intellectual *and* emotional level, the nature of his or her conflicts and feels free, in terms of newfound self-perceptions, to gratify drives in a more mature, conflict-free manner.

Classical psychoanalysis includes the method of free association to promote the determination of causality, establish the transference, and promote insight based on the interpretations derived from the content of the narrative or discourse produced by free associations. Interpretation is, of course, a communication of the psychotherapist's insight to the patient and involves delineating potential meanings of the common denominators discerned in the patient's behavioral patterns. Because this is an exceedingly complex and delicate task, a number of preparatory interventions may be necessary to lay the groundwork or provide evidence before sharing the interpretation with the patient is appropriate. Again, interpretation usually leads to the patient's own perception.

Object-Relations Theory has a greater emphasis on the earliest years of life, and especially the quality of the attachment to and relationship with the mothering-one on the part of the infant/toddler/child. In contrast to classical, Freudian psychoanalysis, Object-Relations Theory gives less emphasis to purely biological and genetic factors. This theory also concerns itself with treating more-severe emotional disorders and has extended psychoanalysis and its application to working with severe personality or character disturbances or even with the psychoses. Additionally, there is an even greater emphasis in Object-Relations Theory on viewing the relationship between patient and psychotherapist as essential to the healing or "curative" aspects of any form of treatment that is undertaken. That is, taking into account the findings of psychoanalytically informed infant-developmental-attachment research, the psychoanalytically oriented Object-Relations Theory or Self-Psychology clinician arrives at an assessment as to the nature of the patient's emotional disregulation. Based on an awareness of the mind (in psychoanalytic terms, the *psychic apparatus)*, the psychoanalytical therapist attempts to provide, in the treatment relationship, a "new edition" of earlier, important relationships (termed *transference)*. The psychotherapist offers, as a new caretaking object to whom the patient attaches, a new opportunity to evoke, confront, and, eventually, work through earlier disruptions to his or her emotional equilibrium. Initially, the patient hands over to the Object-Relations Theory or Self-Psychology therapist, who comes to function as an auxiliary part of the self, certain functions that the patient cannot manage; for example, the capacities for self-soothing, self-calming, and drive regulation. Gradually, under the healing, informative, formative, and transformative aspects of the treatment, the patient is able to first mimic and then manage more and more of these functions autonomously. For these outcomes to be attained, classical psychoanalysts assert that the optimal treatment is intense, conducted by meeting with the patient three to five times per week. In contemporary practice, however, not all patients are willing or able to agree to such intense treatment, so the course of the treatment can involve meeting less frequently across a more extended period of time (usually one session per week). Also, the issue regarding the use of a couch has gradually been accorded far less importance to the establishment of a beneficial psychotherapeutic process. These adjustments to classical psychoanalysis not withstanding, many practitioners of Object-Relations or Self-Psychology would assert that their aims and goals are quite similar to those of classical analysts. Owing to the advancements in theory and technique associated with these innovative perspectives, such clinicians would assert that treatment outcomes associated with contemporary practice compare favorably with those of classical psychoanalysis.

CHAPTER 4

THERAPEUTIC GUIDANCE FROM A DEVELOPMENTAL THEORY

Beginning with Margaret Mahler

Although Dr. Mahler doesn't stand chronologically at the beginning of Developmental Theory's creation, and the theory about to be presented is an amalgam *based on* but not restricted to her contributions, it is an excellent idea to begin with her work.[24] Her ideas were research-based and considered revolutionary at the time she developed them and still seem so to many.[25] Discussion of Mahler's (and others') ideas about *normal* development are discussed below, although there is also discussion about the various things that can go wrong with normal development. We will present a developmental sequence, with *approximate* time periods that lead to the Developmental Period. Note that these time periods overlap in some cases, allowing for individual differences in children and their parents.

Stage 1: Normal Autism A: Birth to One Month

Perhaps William James, America's first psychologist, said it best when he stated that we are born into a "blooming, buzzing confusion."[26] Edith Jacobson later described this

---

24   Many authors like to trace Mahler's ancestors back through Karen Horney, Melanie Klein, other post-Freudians, other members of the "British school," even Anna Freud. Regardless of who Mahler's predecessors may be, we begin with her for two reasons: she clearly describes pre-Oedipal development and her work has an empirical basis.
25   See especially these classical writings: Mahler, M. (1971). A study of the separation-individuation process. *The psychoanalytic study of the child*, 26, 403–424.; Mahler, M., Pine, F., & Bergman, A. (1975). *The psychological birth of the human infant*. New York: Basic Books.
26   James, W. (1890). *Psychology*. New York: Henry Holt.

"confusion" of first consciousness as being like a stream of consciousness.[27] Even a casual student of psychology will recognize both of these theories as being in the "nurture" camp in the age-old nature-versus-nurture debate on human nature that was made famous in the play My Fair Lady.

We know now that theories rigidly privileging a purely environmental ("nature") causal explanation are not completely correct. There *do* seem to be hard-wired (to use one of our popular present-day metaphors) connections in the infant. For example, studies of the eye movements of infants even a few months old show that infants will spend much more time viewing faces in the anatomically correct configuration, as compared to faces with jumbled features or even interesting patterns, sometimes with more complexity.[28] We also know that the infant has a variety of built-in reflexes (so as not to be structureless) such as rooting, sucking, and grasping. All of these reflexes are clearly in the service of forming a life-giving bond with another human being.[29] A few other reflexes (such as the Babinski reflex, which gradually disappears with maturity), however, do not have such a clear connection to bonding.[30] Nonetheless, recognizing that there are some built-in structures, the overall structure of the infant's mind can probably best be characterized as shown in Figure 1 (which many of our critics call our best artistic effort—please forgive the poor joke, as there is no figure below).

Figure 1

Note that what is emphasized in this model is the lack of structure (or, to put it another way, the flexibility and openness to the molding of experience of the young infant).

---

27   Jacobson, E. (1964). *The self and the object world.* New York: International Universities Press.
28   See Fantz, R. L. (1961). The origin of form perception. *Scientific American,* May, 66–72.; Haaf, R. A., Smith, P. H., & Smitley, S. (1983). Infant response to face-like patterns under fixed-trial and infant-control procedure. *Child Development, 54,* 172–177; and Walton, G. E. & Bower, T. G. R. (1993). Newborns form "prototypes" in less than 1 minute. *Psychological Science, 4,* 203–205.
29   Bowlby, J. (1969). *Attachment and loss: Vol. 1. Attachment.* New York: Basic Books; and Rice, R. D. (1975). Premature infants respond to sensory stimulation. American Psychological Association Monitor. Washington: APA.
30   See Lefton, L. A. (1994). *Psychology* (5th ed.). Boston: Allyn and Bacon (pp. 284–285).

Stage 2: Normal Autism B: One to Three Months

As time passes, order comes out of chaos, if by nothing else than the process of association, whereby certain objects and experiences go together. We know from observation that at this time, boundaries that adults take for granted, such as the boundaries of skin (an early, primitive precursor for distinguishing between inner and outer, "me" from "not-me"), can be a surprise to the child, who might bite his toe or finger and then grimace in apparent surprise at the pain.

Some of these connections might seem quite sensible to us from our adult perspectives and common-sensical to the untrained, lay-person's eye—e.g., the (apparently) acquired calming function of a blanket used by the mother to put the child down for rest. Facial expressions in an adult seem to trigger similar facial expressions in children only 36 hours old.[31] These are employed quite "naturally" by parents in their spontaneous interactions with their babies as ways to soothe them and engage with them ("making faces" at the infant, offering a soft toy or blanket, etc.). Facial expressions of caregivers also have been shown to be preferred to those of strangers.[32] However, it is known that during this developmental time frame that the child's mind is especially susceptible to learning by the principle of association (à la Watson). Spurious connections can take on a "meaning" to the child very similar to the bell for Pavlov's dog, even though such experiments also suggest that the child also finds some higher meaning (such as mastery) other than just "feeding" in learning the task of eating.[33] For example, a baby may be lying in its bassinet, just waking up from a snooze. The infant may feel a pleasant warmness infusing its world somewhere. Perhaps, baby looks around the room for a while and looks at a mobile suspended over the bassinet but soon begins to feel uncomfortable. The urine that had caused the pleasant warmth now begins to get cold; the uric acid begins to burn or itch, and the baby starts crying.

If the infant has a reasonably good caregiver,[34] the parent will soon open the door and come in to check, probably cooing as they come, and perhaps Spot will come bounding in behind them (not to be left out of the action). Soon, the baby's parent will discover the problem and make the infant comfortable, and the crying will stop.

---

31   Field, T., Woodson, R., Cohen, D., Garcia, R., & Greenberg, R. (1983). Discrimination and imitation of facial expression by term and pre-term neonates. *Infant Behavior and Development, 6*, 485-490; and Nelson, C. A. & Ludemann, P. M. (1989). Past, current and future trends in infant face perception research. *Canadian Journal of Psychology, 43*, 183-198.

32   Mauer, D. & Salapatek, P. (1976). Developmental changes in the scanning of faces by young infants. *Child Development, 47*, 523-527.

33   Papousek, H. & Papousek, M. (1987). Intuitive parenting: a didactic counterpart to the infant's precocity in integrative capacities. In J. D. Osofsky (Ed.), *Handbook of infant development* (2nd ed.) (pp. 669–720). New York: Wiley.

34   Winnicott, D. W. (1965). The theory of the parent-infant relationship. In *The maturational processes and the facilitating environment* (pp. 37–55). New York: International Universities Press.

From our adult point of view, several actions, people, and objects have interceded in this sequence, but there is no reason to believe that the child has viewed the experience as a combination of many factors, primarily because the child responds to each movement or event with wonder, as if it were a discrete, unconnected event. If the events happen over and over again, however, the child will experience them as an island of organization in the midst of the chaotic stream of existence—*but as an island whose boundaries do not follow adult logic and may well include a parent (or parts of them), Spot, or parts of the self.*

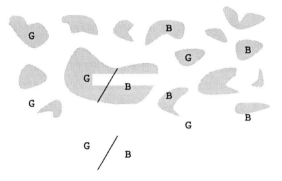

These are like Kernberg's unit of object-relations[35] and are known as ego-nuclei, or selfobject nuclei (see Figure 2). Kernberg notes that these units consist of an image of the object, the self, and a pleasurable or unpleasurable affect that functions as a sort of bridge or connection between the other two images.

Figure 2

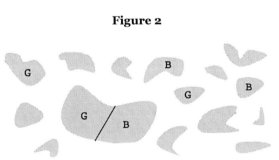

The "B" in this and all later drawings stands for Bad, as in a frustrating object representation or frustrating/uncomfortable selfobject. The "G" in this and all later drawings stands for Good, as in a gratifying objects representation or satisfying/calming selfobject.

35   Kernberg, O. W. (1976). *Object relations theory and clinical psychoanalysis.* New York: Aronson.

Stage 3: Symbiosis

Between three and twelve months of age, depending on the child and circumstances, of all the things that start to "go together" in the infant's mind, "Mother and me" seem to go together most often. Studies have shown that the child's primary caregiver may not be the biological mother, but even when childcare is shared, a special bond seems to form between mother and child. Mahler, following from D. W. Winnicott, describes a time of "primary maternal preoccupation" typical of normal development.

At this stage, stranger-anxiety arises. Before, baby would "go to anyone" because baby did not realize the difference between "anyone" and a caregiver, but now baby is much more choosy. Father may be rejected, although probably preferred to a stranger. Grandmothers, aunts, grandfathers, sisters, and brothers may all fall into the same category as the father, although that is all conditional on the childcare arrangements. Men with beards, if they are unusual in the child's experience to this point, may cause crying; anything that is "strange" can seem threatening, while the familiar caregiver or caregivers can have an immediate and thorough calming effect. Developmental psychologists note that the child does not seem to notice that Mother and child are separate. Certainly, Mother's nipples are not regarded as "not-me," nor is it likely that any other part of a reasonably caring mother will be regarded as "not-me." In fact, one theorist goes so far as to suggest that the child fantasizes that Mother and child are one organism that the child controls.[36] A way of thinking about the child's representation of life is depicted in Figure 3.

Figure 3

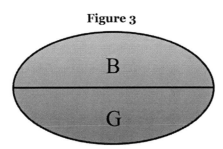

Stage 4: Hatching

If symbiosis goes well and the child learns through the correct empathic responses to the child's needs on the part of the caregiver, the child will soon seek his or her own

---

36   Winnicott, D. W. (1965). Ego distortion in terms of true and false self. In *Maturational processes and the facilitating environment: Studies in the theory of emotional development* (pp. 140–152). New York: International Universities Press.

satisfaction.[37] The earliest signs of this usually are bracing away from Mother and crawling away and checking back. This "hatching" usually begins around seven months of age, sometimes as late as eighteen months. If the caregiver handles this comfortably and doesn't abandon the child (perhaps thinking "There, now the little bugger can take care of herself!"), the child develops more and more independence. Peek-a-boo is a fun game for the child at this point as he or she learns of personal security and the permanency of caregivers.[38]

Unfortunately, Mahler uses words in her explanation of this stage that have proven confusing for many people: Mahler postulates that two processes are occurring simultaneously—individuation and separation.[39] *Individuation* refers to the refinement of mastery skills, but *separation* refers to the child's ability to remain comfortably and securely separate. Both individuation and separation must be nurtured and developed in parallel or the child will be clingy and not able to reach the next stage of development. Figure 4 is a pictorial representation of the self-system at this stage. The Gs and Bs are circled in this and the next stage to represent part-objects, which are a child's (or later, perhaps, a patient's) internal experiences of a person as all-frustrating or malevolent (bad object) or as all-satisfying or gratifying (good object).

Stage 5: Practicing

As early as the beginning of the second year and as late as the beginning of the third year of life, the child becomes increasingly skilled at manipulating her social and material environment. As she becomes more and more secure in being separate, she enters a "love affair" with the world, as if "the world is her oyster," and she almost can't get enough of her play *apart* from the caregiver. The caregiver seems to be ignored, although observation has shown that this is only appearance. It is as if the child enters a period of "normal narcissism," in which she acts as if she needs no one else, but if the caregiver is removed, the child begins to act dejected, depressed, and then angry. She may even reject the caregiver upon his or her return. The caregiver is needed for reflection, much like a mirror functions, to confer reality upon the child's achievements a sense of guidance and a feeling of safety. Figure 5 is a pictorial portrayal of this self-system.

---

37   Ainsworth, M. D. S. (1979). Infant-mother attachment. *American Psychologist, 34,* 932–937.; Sroufe, L. A. (1983). Infant-caregiver attachment and patterns of adaptation in pre-school: The roots of maladaption and competence. In M. Perlmutter (Ed.), *Minnesota symposium in child psychology* (pp. 41–83), 16. Hillsdale, NJ: Erlbaum.
38   Piaget, J. (1963). The attainment of invariants and reversible operations in the development of thinking. *Social Research, 30,* 283–299.
39   Mahler, M., Pine, F., & Bergman, A. (1975). *The psychological birth of the human infant.* New York: Basic Books.

Figure 4

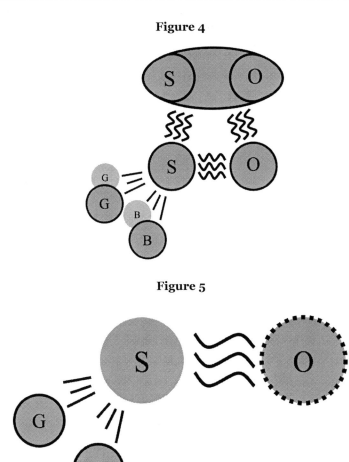

Figure 5

Stage 6: Rapprochement

Whether the child gets enough of the trials and tribulations that life may send her way, simply gets enough of her own independent power, or some combination of the two, she eventually realizes that she does better when bonded to an adult. Between eighteen months and thirty-six months of age, she seems to oscillate between connectedness and independence. Before, the child seemed to ignore the caregiver purposefully and indefatigably. The intensity of this apparent disregard dissipates, and the child seems to regain interest in the caregiver, even treating him or her like a *person*. The drives toward separation and individuation remain, however, as does the fear of symbiotic re-engulfment (which would defeat at least separation, and perhaps both separation *and* individuation), so the child is back and forth between bonding and maintaining distance. Figure 6 represents this self-state.

Figure 6

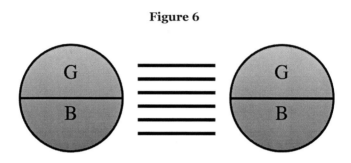

Stage 7: The Door to the Oedipal Period

As affect becomes more neutralized (not so all-or-nothing) and the child becomes more secure as an independent creature (usually between 3 and 3 1/2 years), stability really sets in, and the child senses both her own and her caregiver's (love-object) constancy. These developments allow the child to risk forming tangible connections with third parties (to become triadic) for the first time. Note that in Stages 3 through 6, the child was almost exclusively dyadic (a two-person self-system). Father, or a substitute, serves as a safe harbor to draw the child out of the dyadic system, as the "ambassador to the larger world." Figure 7 portrays this new self-organization.

Affect

Though nothing has been said about affect until now, it could have been addressed from the beginning. It appears that there is some structure to early emotion,[40] although it is largely chaotic and mostly learned, as is postulated in Schachter and Singer's landmark experiment.[41] Even from the beginning, however, emotions appear to be organized largely around pain (feeling bad) and pleasure (feeling good). The dividing lines in Figures 3 through 6 are supposed to represent these two major feelings or self-states. Observations of early childhood almost universally show that children display extreme expressions of

---

40   Tronick, E. Z. (1989). Emotions and emotional communication in infants. *American Psychologist, 44*, 112–119.
41   Schachter, S. & Singer, J. E. (1962). Cognitive, social and physiological determinants of emotional state. *Psychological Review, 69*, 379–399.

these two emotions, depending on the children's comfort or discomfort. More specifically, when an infant is upset, it tends to get red in the face, have distended nostrils, show teeth or gums, clench fists (moving them back and forth, even impacting anything in the way), and kick its legs. If we saw this in an adult male, we might run for cover from what looked like a total rage reaction.

Figure 7

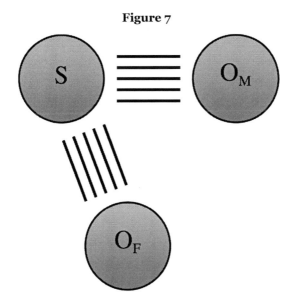

Conversely, if the infant is satisfied, it appears as if all memory of the bad feelings disappear: The child's face becomes smooth and calm, there may be a broad smile, and normal color returns; we have even heard parents confess jealousy about how calm the child appears. In particular, one said "Look, she looks so peaceful and angelic, almost like the face of Buddha. I wish I could get that peaceful."

Some theorists argue that the early ego-nuclei are formed around either pain or pleasure. Others state that within the symbiotic state, the child feels good and experiences the outside or "not-me" as dangerous or feeling bad.

During the hatching and practicing stages, matters become more complex for the child, with good and bad feeling states splitting off, both within and without. About the time of rapprochement, we begin to see in the child the apportionment of complex experience states into all-good and all-bad part-objects to render such potentially overwhelming experiences manageable. At the time of rapprochement, extreme emotional states begin to be integrated and neutralized, finally reaching fairly stable integration in Stage 7. The intermodal exchange of affective signals from the infant to the mother and back again—

accompanied by such things as mimicking of facial expressions, sounds, etc.—leads to the infant securing a sense of existing, as it were, concretely, through the regulatory responses secured from the mother. In more abstract terms, the infant (and later, as maturing toddler) comes to feel that it exists because it locates itself as being "held" in time and space—including across time and space—as in the mind of the [m]other. This represents a growing, multifaceted complexity of development that, among other things, lays the groundwork for the differentiation of self from other to come.

A Developmental Theory or a Psychotherapeutic Theory?

The earlier verbiage about the obstructiveness of the theories under discussion notwithstanding, it will be important to tie each of the enumerated stages of our model to some basic forms of psychopathology. Not all forms of psychopathology will be covered, for some are better related to later developmental stages, as will be shown later. Furthermore, it is important to realize that these pathological states will not mean the turning of normal development into psychopathology; rather, Developmental Theory will form a model of the mind to organize these difficulties around, either as a result of deficits that prevent a child from fully developing beyond a stage, as traumas that block further development temporarily or as foundations for jumping off into deviations.[42] In all cases, however, the stage of development will be shown to provide important and basic methods of understanding psychopathologies, and the corresponding theory will also provide basic blueprints for proper therapeutic responses that seem related to these stages.

Although much has already been written about Oedipal and post-Oedipal crises and their accompanying psychopathology, later sections of this book will also sketch a similar connection between these developments and resultant psychopathology, showing that they bear some striking resemblances to one another.

Throughout the following chapters, remember that a theory is just a theory: Similarity—and even predictability—do not necessarily imply causality. Instead, our attempt will be to use our Developmental Theory in the service of having workable and understandable therapeutic techniques for a wide range of mental health problems. Chapter 6 will address these connections directly.

---

42   Gedo, J. E., & Goldberg, A. (1973). *Models of the Mind: A Psychoanalytic Theory*. University of Chicago Press.

CHAPTER 5

THE DIFFERENCE BETWEEN OBJECT-RELATIONS THEORY AND SELF-PSYCHOLOGY

F reud's theories are reputedly derived in part from his primary patient population of middle-class Viennese Jewish women of the 19th and early 20th centuries. Object-Relations Theory developed, for the most part, in pre- and post-World War II Britain by people who began their careers as psychoanalysts. The patients being seen were either children or seriously disturbed adults whom many others regarded as untreatable. Self-Psychology originated at the Institute for Psychoanalysis in Chicago in the 1960s with adult patients who were screened out for psychoanalysis because of severe character disorders. Consequently, one difference between Self-Psychology and Object-Relations Theory is that the former is retrospective (that is, it recreates the developmental history from the memory of, and experience with, the adult). Although some Object-Relations theorists had primarily treated adult populations, many other very influential Object-Relations theorists worked with children. Accordingly, these theorists' (psychoanalysts') view of development and associated psychopathological adjustments was based on "real time" observations; that is, *as it happened.*

Furthermore, in working with children, one often becomes involved in milieu therapy or external (even behavioral) manipulations that would be administered in the context of solid relationships. Another difference between Self-Psychology and Object-Relations Theory is that Self-Psychology typically involves face-to-face psychotherapy. Although it arose directly from and clearly employs concepts and words from classical psychoanalysis, Object-Relations Theory has been regarded by some theorists as not being a form of psychoanalytic thinking (and certainly not of psychoanalytic treatment methodology). The idea that it is not psychoanalytic thinking is especially curious because many of the pivotal characters in the development of the "Independent" or "British" School (terms that have been applied to the Object-Relations practitioners) and in the field of Self-Psychology have placed themselves firmly within the fold of psychoanalysis.[43]

The external focus of Object-Relations theorists led to *more* of an emphasis on relationships (interpersonal focus) in that camp. Although Self-Psychology also uses many words and concepts borrowed from psychoanalysis, it has more of an internal (intrapsychic) focus than does Object-Relations Theory, its experiential portion coming almost exclusively from face-to-face psychotherapy.[44]

Traditional Freudian psychoanalytic thinking had a place for both the internal (analyzing conflicts, for example) and for the external (the concepts of transference and counter-transference). The focus on the internal was probably stronger, with much attention given to drives, libido, the id, the ego, and the superego, but there was also a place for understanding what took place in the relationship. Self-Psychology and Object-Relations Theory have broadened the use of the relationship as both a diagnostic and therapeutic tool and have also introduced us to a variety of previously unknown transferences and compelling counter-transferences that might be better labeled as "the patient's pull." That is, the patient tends to present with and evoke particular reactions and affects within and across both members of the psychoanalytic pair, based upon the potential for the treatment to re-awaken and heighten frozen internal states, developmental arrests and fixations. Both theories view such counter-transferences as having little to nothing to do with unanalyzed conflicts in the psychotherapist (as counter-transference would mean in traditional psychoanalysis), and taught us how to work with these relationship factors.

---

43   Some (John Bowlby, for example) have been asked or told to leave the "orthodox" psychoanalytic circles, as well as, being accused of going "too far" or of having beliefs about human functioning that were not in keeping with orthodox psychoanalysis.

44   Both theories have been accused of being far too external and interpersonal and of having lost their true psychoanalytic roots because of an alleged exclusive emphasis on the relationship and a disregard for internal conflict between parts of the personality. (See Murray, Ibid.) If one examines a review of Kohut's contribution to defense and resistance, such as Oremland, J. D. [(1985). Kohut's reformulation of defense and resistance as applied to therapeutic psychoanalysis, in Goldberg, A. (Ed.), *Progress in self-psychology (Vol. 1)* (pp. 97–105). New York: The Guilford Press.], one is tempted to agree with Murray, for Oremland leaves the reader feeling that everything should be seen as interpersonal. In the same volume, however, M. Shane, in his article entitled "Summary of Kohut's 'The Self-Psychological Approach to Defense and Resistance' " (pp. 69–79), leaves the reader to understand that the therapist using Self-Psychology "is able to broaden his perspective beyond this mechanistic view" (p. 69), meaning that Self-Psychology is meant to be a *correction* of, rather than a replacement for, traditional psychoanalytic thinking.

Shane also makes the point that Kohut speaks of a self that may experience attack and respond with defenses to promote survival. Again, the implication is that Kohut's thought, however radically parts of it might be used by some as a substitute for Freudian theory, leaves plenty of room for intrapsychic study.

Most prominent thinkers in both camps show at least some interest in retaining concepts from traditional psychoanalysis, such as those having to do with drives and intrapsychic conflict.[45]

Sharing much common language has proven to be a mixed blessing for psychoanalytical professionals, theorists, and scholars, for although it appears that the three theories are often addressing the same subjects in the same way, one quickly learns that the same word can be used by different thinkers to mean quite different things. Even within the British School or within Self-Psychology the same word may have important differences in meaning depending on who is uttering the word in which context. Reading original writings can therefore be somewhat hazardous and can require careful research on the part of the reader to pin down exactly what is meant by each key word depending on the writer.

With all the above said and done, it still seems that the two new theories, at least, converge and have much in common in many ways; sometimes the categories or descriptors are different,[46] but the overall developmental lines and many of the major concepts seem to be remarkably similar. It is almost as if two different camps of researchers, using different samples and different methods, derived theories that are *very* compatible. Many people use the terms for the two schools almost interchangeably and graft concepts from one onto the other, primarily because they are so similar that it is easy to do.

Although both the new theories share the concept of trauma and developmental arrest with traditional psychoanalysis, they introduce a new concept that is not directly addressed in psychoanalytic thought: that of *structural deficit*. The idea behind structural deficit is that a person may have a problem not because of some version of post-traumatic stress syndrome, perhaps with its own development through the years of symbolic symptoms, but because a necessary part of his or her personality (such as the ability to calm oneself) did not develop. The Self-Psychologists and Object-Relations theorists point out many examples of "faulty" primary relationships and talk of situations in which a deficient parent "teaches" his child deficient behavior. This important theoretical

---

45   A few theorists who claim they retain the concepts of the original psychoanalytic tradition include Winnicott, Jacobson, Kohut, and Kernberg. One might wonder, as many have, where the examples of traditional concepts in their treatments are, and one might wonder that even more with some of these theorists' students. In contrast, a few "pure" Object-Relations theorists (such as Fairbairn) openly admit that the "new" theory supplants the "classical" psychoanalytic theory in their minds and practices. St. Clair (2004) reviews these currents and trends within the psychoanalytical movement (one strand or group claiming to build on already-established psychoanalytical theory, and the other purportedly charting an entirely new course).

46   For example, when Kohut describes the merger transference of the narcissistic personality, one may note striking similarities to the description of borderline personality, or intermediate (*à la* Winnicott) relationships, as described by Object-Relations therapists.

difference leads to differences in therapeutic style between traditional psychoanalytical theory and the two newer theories. In the newer psychotherapies, the psychotherapist may temporarily perform the missing function (like an alter ego), may model the function so that it can be taken in by some process of internalization, or may simply use directive psycho-educational approaches with the patient. (It should be emphasized that these elements are also quintessentially psychoanalytical.) Although present even in so-called traditional psychoanalytical theory and treatment, such adjustments to technique have been unnecessarily encumbered with a view of the psychotherapist maintaining an almost surgical objectivity from the patient—one that does not even accord with Freud's actual treatment of his own patients.[47]

In summary, though there are important differences in origin, shadings of variation in emphasis, and distinct terminologies (or use of the same terminologies to mean distinctive things), the similarities and compatibilities of Object-Relations Theory and Self-Psychology seem to greatly outnumber the divergences. The disjunctures (other than language) between them, especially regarding their roots in psychoanalysis, are therefore more difficult to assess, it seems to us. As a result, in this book (and increasingly elsewhere), use of the label defining one field is taken to *include* the other. Where distinctions need to be made, they must be spelled out. This can be especially nettlesome for clinicians, interestingly enough, when discussing theoretical and clinical matters with colleagues who assign different meanings (and therefore clinical, psychological processes) while operating under the impression that everyone knows what everyone is talking about.

---

47   See Freud, S. (1910). *The future prospects of psychoanalytic therapy.* The standard edition of the complete psychological works of Sigmund Freud (Vol. 11). New York: W. W. Norton. London: Hogarth Press, 1953. (See especially pp. 139–151.)

CHAPTER 6

FINDING A METHOD TO THE MADNESS

The Diagnostic and Statistical Manual for Mental Disorders, Fourth Edition, Text Revision (DSM-IV-TR (2000)[48]) lists the following characteristic symptoms for schizophrenia:

1. Delusions
2. Hallucinations
3. Disorganized speech (e.g., frequent derailment or incoherence)
4. Grossly disorganized or catatonic behavior
5. Negative symptoms (i.e., affective flattening, alogia, or avolition).

Other texts have historically listed such symptoms as loose associations; thought broadcasting; ideas of reference; inability to care for the basic needs of the self; grandiosity; hyperconcern with good, evil, and sex; a type of speech described as a "word salad"[49]; disorientation to place, time, or person; thought disorder; labile affect; poor reality testing; and others.[50]

Certainly, either of the above lists is interesting, yet how do we make sense of such a collection, or even a partial collection of such symptoms? Biochemical theories and cybernetic theories have attempted to explain at least some of the symptoms, as have other theories, such as Object-Relations Theory.

How does Object-Relations Theory understand schizophrenia? First we should note that many of the earliest Object-Relations Theorists worked primarily with the psychotic

---

48   American Psychiatric Association. (2000). *Diagnostic and statistical manual of mental disorders* (4th ed.), Text Revision (p. 312). Washington, D.C.: Author.
49   A phrase that has been used to describe certain aspects of the schizophrenics' speech.
50   See list in Lefton, Ibid. pp. 523–526 as a typical list in a popular introductory textbook.

and with patients with what would today be called personality disorders. Their theories are uniquely relevant to these difficult populations.[51] Before Object-Relations Theory, psychotic conditions and personality disorders used to be considered beyond the reach of traditional psychoanalysis and were called unanalyzable until the birth of psychoanalytic psychotherapy. This was largely spurred on by the contributions of post-Freudians such as the Object-Relations practitioners and Self-Psychologists.[52]

It is also helpful to note that in the DSM-IV-TR list above, no terms apply specifically to the paranoid type of schizophrenia (which has its own diagnostic criteria), nor to the hebephrenic or a few other subtypes.[53] Most experts these days believe that there is more than one type of schizophrenia, yet no one can offer a unified theory that predicts such strange psychotic symptoms or explains their existence. Object-Relations Theory offers explanations that are therapeutically useful because they focus on working with these difficult groups, generating techniques in addition to medication and environmental management.

Looking back at our developmental model, imagine a person stuck (arrested), through either deficit or trauma, at Developmental Stage 2 or 3. Note that at either of these stages, the boundaries we commonly accept as adults are not established. Note further that connections that mature adults might regard as spurious are present in the ego-nuclei of Stage 2. For example, if the infant were able to verbalize about the diaper-changing example given in Chapter 4, he might present us with what we would regard as a "word salad" consisting of phrases such as "burn," "Spot," "mobile," "Mamma," "crying," and "feel better." Maybe we would hear it as "Burning Spot mobile Mamma crying feel better." It would be amazing if anyone could make sense of such a collection of words, although some have suggested that we might do so with a thorough examination of the patient's history and exhaustive interviews with the family.[54] In Scenario 1 in Chapter 1, Mel appears to have done something like this in the course of his regular work with Joe.

Might not an "arrest" of some sort at Stage 2 or 3 explain why people believe in systems of meaning that have no consensual validation? Might not this also explain the poor reality testing, the triggering of one sensory event by another seemingly unrelated event (hallucination), or the lack of organization of a person with schizophrenia? One

51   For thorough discussions of this issue, see: St. Clair, M. (2004). *Object Relations and self-psychology: An introduction* (4th ed.). Monterey, CA: Brooks/Cole.; and Summers, F. S. (1994). *Object relations theories and psychopathology.* New York: The Analytic Press.
52   For a summary discussion of the issue, see Basch, M. (1988). *Understanding psychotherapy: The science behind the art.* New York: Basic Books, Inc. (specifically, pp. 309–311)
53   Lefton, Ibid., pp. 524–526.
54   As one example, see Ettinger, B., Telerand, A., Kronenberg, Y., & Gaoni, B. (1991). Verbal hallucinations in psychotic patients. *Israel Journal of Psychiatry and Related Sciences, 28*(2), 39–49.

author even goes so far as to quote W.R. Bion's theories and suggests that the experience of the hallucination is preferable to the anxiety or over-stimulation that the patient would otherwise experience.[55] If we were to assume that the emotional development of such an individual was along the lines of a child six months old, would we continue to be surprised that the person could not care for himself or make sense of his environment?

Remember that affect seems to start in a rather all-or-nothing "feeling good or feeling bad" state; one would therefore not be surprised at the *lability* of affect. If a person with schizophrenia had some sense of his or her vulnerability and attempted to defend him- or herself by holding in affect and disorganization, the psychotherapist would not be surprised at the presence of flat affect, which would make the patient appear defensive to the outside world.

Going back a step, some psychodynamic explanations have attempted to explain autism as an organization of the self like that of Stage 2, but with a *deanimated frozen wall*[56] around it. We do know that people with autism, like young children at Stage 2, are mesmerized by sensory experiences; clanging rhymes (clang sounds); repetitive visual, tactual, or auditory experiences; and the like. The deanimated frozen wall is a premature defensive structure whereby the individual has separated in a protective way before he or she can be differentiated from the mothering-one, for example, as a separate person (to use Mahler's terminology). Consequently, we are dealing with a theory of autism or of schizophrenia that is not "pathologizing" normal development.[57] Something has gone "haywire,"[58] and the incomplete self-structure is sealed in with a precocious wall of separation.[59] At least the crucial symptoms of autism and schizophrenia can be well explained by the notion of the deanimated frozen wall.

55   Ferro, A. (1993). From hallucination to dream: From evacuation to the tolerability of pain in the analysis of a preadolescent. *Psychoanalytic Review, 80*(3), 389–404.

56   See page 309 of Mahler, M. S., Pine, F., & Bergman, A. (1963). Thoughts about development and individuation. *Psychoanalytic Study of the Child, 18,* 307–324.

57   See St. Clair, Ibid., and Summers (secondary sources and therefore much more readable) for summary explanations of Otto Kernberg's famous criticism of Melanie Klein's theory on the grounds that she "pathologizes" normal development by including stages involving normal paranoia.

58   For evidence that something is definitely amiss in the early Object-Relations of schizophrenics, see Bell, M., Lysaker, P., & Milstein, R. (1992). Object-Relations deficits in subtypes of schizophrenia. *Journal of Clinical Psychology, 48*(4), 433–444.

59   Articles in which this approach is described include Kates, M. & Rockland, L. H. (1994). Supportive psychotherapy of the schizophrenic patient. Special section: Supportive psychotherapy. *American Journal of Psychotherapy, 48*(4), 543–561.; Kotcher, M. & Smith, T. E. (1993). Three phases of Clozapine treatment and phase-specific issues for patients and families. *Hospital and Community Psychiatry, 44*(8), 744–747.; Kline, J., Becker, J., & Giese, C. (1992). Psychodynamic interventions revisited: Options for the treatment of schizophrenia. *Psychotherapy, 29*(3), 366–377; and Leff, J. (1992). Schizophrenia and similar conditions. *International Journal of Mental Health, 21*(2), 25–40.

Note further that the treatment of choice for schizophrenia is not psychoanalysis, gestalt psychotherapy, Rogerian psychotherapy, psychodynamic psychotherapy, or even supportive psychotherapy, but a combined treatment approach of modified psychoanalytical psychotherapy that incorporates *management and direction*. This treatment is accomplished through medication, in a hospital milieu, or on an outpatient basis, much like parents are instructed to provide for a child with autism.[60] Empathically repeating back the nonsense syllables of the child of six months, as we might do in a hospital milieu or as employed in Rogerian psychotherapy, would do little for the child; the parent must make sense of the child's world for the child and manage it. We do the same thing for patients with schizophrenia.

Some research also shows that for the person with schizophrenia, the self has no special position in the world of objects[61] and so, needs the management of a caring other to make his or her world cohesive, much like an infant needs the care of a loving parent for the same reasons.

Counter-transference Reactions and Psychotherapeutic Techniques

The psychotherapist of someone with schizophrenia feels exquisitely like a caregiving parent of a young child. The patient is so helpless, vulnerable, and discouraged that, in many ways, he or she emotionally resembles a child.

All successful techniques for treating schizophrenia entail "parental" management of the behavior and emotional equilibrium of the patient. They typically also include feeding the patient the correct substances[62] to produce calm and directed energy. The clinician managing the patient's environment for safety and comfort, and serving as an intermediary to help the patient achieve his goals, much like the management of a young child, is paramount for the successful treatment of schizophrenia. Mel, in Scenario 1 of Chapter 1, illustrates the psychodynamic portion of this kind of treatment.

To establish contact with an autistic patient, psychotherapists will use rhythms and sensory experiences to attract the patient's attention, much as they would to build a connection to children in Stage 2. Talking to the child with autism about what mother or father might have done or using a psychodynamic technique would not help.

If we were to theorize that a person with paranoid schizophrenia was someone "trapped" in Stage 3, perhaps again with a defensive deanimated frozen wall around her,

---

60   See references for footnote 56.
61   Kafka, J. S. (1990). On the question of insight in psychosis. Special issue: Psychoanalysis and severe emotional illness. *Journal of the American Academy of Psychoanalysis, 18*(1), 18–28.
62   Symbolically, the psychotherapist's presence. More literally, the "feed," while still symbolic, might involve the patient "feeding on/taking in" the psychotherapist's words; or taking a medication.

we would realize that she would be riddled with fear of anything even remotely strange and would feel safe only with an accepted caregiver. The best treatment for a person with paranoid schizophrenia thus matches what is learned from the developmental theory learned from Mahler's work: One person should carefully establish a trusting, caring bond with the patient and help the patient safely meet her adaptive needs, regulate herself, make sense of her world, and defend against bad feelings.

Applying the same logic to Stage 4, we would see that a person developmentally arrested or fixated at this stage would be "trapped" into prematurely attempting individuality, while at the same time oscillating back into a state of merger. We would also see that such a person would not yet be able to integrate good and bad feeling states and so would have to resort to splitting them off into good and bad part states. Conflicts about autonomy, splitting, loss of boundaries, and merger and difficulty interpreting reality in an objective fashion are all hallmarks of the borderline personality (which will be elaborated on in Chapter 8).

Being stuck at Stage 5 would leave a person in a state of hyper-individuality (at least for appearance's sake) yet highly vulnerable to the absence of a caretaking object who could appreciate, guide, limit, and protect. Though personal grandiosity would mark the person, theory would predict that this "self-esteem" would be quite fragile. Furthermore, if the self-system were to break down, the person would be at the mercy of powerful "all-or-nothing" feeling states that would lead to either rage or bliss. These characteristics are typical of the Narcissistic Personality Disorder (see Chapter 7 for further discussion). A good-enough parent of a child in Stage 5 at the "normal" age would be present at a protective distance, appreciative of the child's efforts, and offering a model of mastery. Furthermore, this parent would not be overly interfering. These parental strategies would form a facilitative basic approach to dealing with Narcissistic Personality Disorder, as well.

The deanimated frozen wall around Stage 6 would leave the person feeling whole and seeing others as whole, but also beset by marked mood swings. If the predominance of the experiences were in the direction of feeling bad, the mood swings would tilt in the direction of depression, but if the predominance were in the direction of feeling good, the swings would be predominately manic. In either of these cases, the self-system would be a personality organization, quite stable over time, much like what we find with bipolar personality disorders.

At Stage 7, the "normal" child would finally be capable of tolerating more than a dyadic system and could form rivalrous bonds, much like the Oedipal child or individual. Again, if the child were defensively "stuck" at this stage, the good parent would help her work out these rivalries at both an internal and external level, much like a psychotherapist (using transference and life events) might help a neurotic patient.

More can be said of the later developments and how deficits that leave a person stuck at those stages would appear and how they could be helped, but the above paragraphs at least illustrate the usefulness of applying a developmental theory embedded within Object-Relations and Self-Psychology to the understanding of the developmental fixations associated with certain psychopathologies, some of which have been previously regarded as untreatable, or which have been seen as treatable by trial-and-error alone.

The coming chapters will focus particularly on several of the pre-Oedipal stages, showing how the manifest symptoms of adult patients can be understood, and indicating a good general psychotherapeutic stance that would be extrapolated from good-enough parenting. Note that the early stages require primarily behavioral stances; the middle stages require a mixture of empathy, interpretation, and management; and the later stages follow the more traditional path of psychoanalytical interpretation and confrontation. As stated before, Object-Relations Theory has an appropriate place for each psychotherapeutic stance, depending on the theory-derived diagnosis of the condition and the associated understanding of the good-enough parenting technique that would fuel the child to achieve the next level of development.

It is also worth mentioning that neither Object-Relations Theory nor Self–Psychology negate the concept of neural biochemistry as an important factor in psychosis, as mentioned in Chapter 1. Just as we know that the stomach lining becomes inflamed and irritated when a person is angry and we know that more epinephrine is discharged when a person senses danger (causing a faster heart rate and other physiological responses), brain chemistry is certainly affected as well. Chronic confusion, for example, would have to have effects on the brain chemistry, like any chronic condition would have on the body. Which comes first—the neurology or the psychosocial factors—may vary with the individual. There is strong evidence now in both the neurological and the psychosocial camps to lead to the "vulnerability" hypothesis.[63] Object-Relations Theory and Self-Psychology do not propose one primary cause of psychosis but state that it appears that some people, whether because of familial, social, or organic factors, are more prone to developing schizophrenia under stress. Research into all causal factors and the search for agents that ameliorate schizophrenia is important, regardless of how schizophrenia develops.

---

63   For discussions of these issues, see Lefton, Ibid., pp. 529–530, and Waslylenki, D. A. (1992). Psychotherapy of schizophrenia revisited. Annual meeting of the Canadian Psychiatric Association. *Hospital and Community Psychiatry, 43*(2), 123–127.

At the same time, as the Kandel articles referenced in Chapter 3 illustrate, psychotherapeutic applications could well produce changes in serotonin levels or other neural chemistry. It is also worthy of mention that people with schizophrenia face dangers with defenses that are quite different from normal or "neurotic" defenses: Schizophrenia causes a person to be afraid, quite literally, of disintegration. When a person with schizophrenia fears falling apart, it is not a figure of speech: his internal world would become incomprehensible and confusing, or he would cease to be as an entity to himself. People with schizophrenia also fear control or domination by a bad object (which would then make them bad as well), so issues concerning good and evil are often on their minds; defenses used include delusions, hallucinations, withdrawal into an isolated world that may appear bizarre to others, becoming repellent to others, etc. This illustrates the need to use different techniques with this disorder, because of the diverse nature of the presenting and/or underlying problem(s) and the type of defenses mobilized.[64]

---

64   For a cogent discussion of this very issue, see: Little, M. (1966). Transference in borderline states. *International Journal of Psycho-Analysis, 47*, 476–485.

CHAPTER 7

HOW DO THE DSM-IV-TR AXIS I SYMPTOMATOLOGIES FIT IN?

At times, individuals report that they discern some correspondence between the classifications of Object-Relations Theory and Self-Psychology and the diagnostic categories of Axis II of the DSM-IV-TR. This is because there is a passing similarity based on a few of the types of personality disorders included in the DSM-IV-TR and those that have often been the focus of psychoanalytical enquiry and refinements in treatment over the years (for instance, Borderline Personality Disorder and Narcissistic Personality Disorder). This is illusory, however, as few can see how the categories of Axis I in any way converge with the classifications of these theories. This is because the theories we are discussing are basically structuralist models of the mind. Axis I describes the symptoms or outward signs that a person might possess. Sometimes practitioners conclude that if a person meets the criteria for an Axis I diagnosis, some deeper entity, like a disease or a syndrome, has been detected. In some cases, such as in the case of bipolar disorder or schizophrenia, there may in fact be an underlying structural problem to the person's personality. These disorders tend to be enduring (although with proper treatment they can be made to disappear) and to possess constellations of characteristics that suggest basic structural deficits in the organization of the self.

The personality disorders of Axis II may have been affected in some degree by the thinking of Self-Psychologists and Object-Relations theorists, but in no way did such practitioners write this Axis. As such, we might regard it as incomplete; there is room for additional categories to be named in the Not-Otherwise-Signified (NOS) class, but whole new families may be added in the future.

The real difference is more fundamental. Whereas DSM-IV-TR is really a nosology of mental disorders named by a committee of experts (informed by history, research, and training) without theoretic underpinnings, the two theories that are under consideration in this book have a much more ambitious aim. DSM-IV-TR is the work of pragmatic experts seeking to construct a system that everyone, from every theoretical persuasion, can use. Note, however, that unlike the *Merck Manual*,[65] another medical reference book that also contains a nosology of diseases, DSM-IV-TR usually makes no attempt to describe the etiology of the disorders or to describe appropriate treatments (growing out of an understanding of the disorder). Object-Relations Theory and Self-Psychology are more like the *Merck Manual*, in that they *do* attempt to describe the causes of the disorders they name and to prescribe at least the basic parameters of treatment based on an understanding of causes. Practitioners in these two theories would generally tend to see the Axis I descriptions of DSM-IV-TR as portraits of how individuals uniquely display the results of their underlying structural defects. In keeping with the times, DSM-IV-TR devotes about twice as much space to problems relating to various forms of chemical dependency (which is a popular way to think these days), whereas a more psychoanalytical thinker would be inclined to agree with the conclusions of the author of *Substance Abuse As a Symptom*,[66] which state that one person lacking in self-esteem might seek to alleviate his distress by using substances, while another might become depressed, another might become anxious, or still another might develop some other condition.

For example, Attention Deficit Disorder with Hyperactivity (ADHD) is a popular contemporary diagnosis (much like Minimal Brain Dysfunction was several years ago), and practitioners make this diagnosis after simply noting concentration difficulties and poor grades, completing checklists, or using any variety of other methods. Furthermore, if one of the stimulants commonly used to help this condition (such as Ritalin, Cylert, or Dexedrine) seems to produce a positive difference, the practitioner, patient, and family all tend to conclude that the diagnosis is confirmed. The logic employed in making a diagnosis following the use of the psychoactive drugs is *not* scientific; it is well known that these stimulants will help even normal persons concentrate better and get higher grades in school. The reasoning is circular, at best. Furthermore, in our own clinical experience, when a person is studied more carefully and deeply, perhaps even with psychological testing employed, one often finds that the difficulties with concentration come from depression, posttraumatic effects, anxiety, or a variety of other conditions. Sometimes,

---

65   Berkow, R. (Ed.). (1977). *The Merck manual of diagnosis and therapy.* Rahway, NJ: Merck & Co.
66   Berger, L. S. (1991). *Substance abuse as a symptom.* Hillsdale, NJ: The Analytic Press.

the psycho-stimulant triggers strong outbursts of anger or even makes the person worse, while an antidepressant improves the person's concentration and reduces his or her agitation.

Object-Relations theorists and Self-Psychologists find Axis I of the DSM-IV-TR somewhat frustrating in that it rarely offers an understanding of a condition (again, the potential causal factors), let alone suggestions for how that condition might be alleviated. Furthermore, Axis I appears to be a (superficial) patchwork of symptoms, symptom clusters, and what are probably actual disorders of the self (such as bipolar disorder, as mentioned above). At the same time, Axis II is frustrating in that it does not seem to go far enough and, furthermore, often uses the same words (but with different meanings) as those used by the theories under consideration in this book.

DSM-IV-TR may be useful because it establishes some common ground for communication and problem solving with other mental health professionals.[67] It also describes a number of conditions that seem to have enduring characteristics. It is also essential for the practitioner to use if he or she wishes to aid his client in achieving some insurance reimbursement, but DSM-IV-TR is hardly the first and last word on psycho-diagnosis and etiological considerations to practitioners using these two theories. Indeed, psychoanalytical theorists and practitioners remain tremendously skeptical of the DSM enterprise, seeing it as an over-simplified, superficial, symptom-focused, "cookbook" approach to incredibly nuanced psychological issues and processes.[68]

---

67   It is well within the tradition of Emil Kraepelin [(1907). *Clinical psychiatry: A textbook for students and physicians* (A. R. Diefendorf, Trans.). New York: Macmillan. (Original work published 1883)] who described syndromes that had been observed by more than one doctor and gave these diagnostic labels. Previous to this, we had only the labels of other systems of thought (such as that coming from the theory of the "humours" of man) or no labels at all, so that practitioners had to speak to each other as if they were encountering something for the first time. Still, even with DSM-IV-TR, one of the appendices makes note of a large list of mental health labels in use somewhere in the world but not part of DSM-IV-TR.

68   Even the efforts of psychoanalysts to devise and codify their own psycho-diagnostic manual, published as the *Psychodynamic Diagnostic Manual,* or PDM (published by the Alliance of Psychoanalytic Organisations in 2006), has met with considerable skepticism. Although it contains more descriptive and phenomenological criteria to aid in classifying various disturbed mental states, the issue comes down to this: Do we really need yet another cookbook? Many practitioners, even in the psychoanalytic camp, have responded in the negative.

CHAPTER 8

THE MYSTIQUE OF THE BORDERLINE

W e do not have enough time to get into a full history of diagnosis and the ways Borderline Personality Disorder has been regarded; it is sufficient for our purposes to know that the borderline disorder has been regarded as either "borderline between psychotic and neurotic"[69] or as a collection or wastebasket of psychoneurotic symptoms that fit no other psychiatric category neatly.[70] Since Freud's time, the borderline condition has had several names and has been considered untreatable (as was mentioned in Chapter 5), meaning that little was discussed concerning these "character neuroses." In recent history, however, Borderline Personality Disorder has received much more attention.

It is difficult to successfully treat patients who have a borderline disorder, so much attention has been given to understanding both the disorder and the therapeutic approach needed for it. Sometimes, after a *very* promising start, the patient is eventually "discharged" or referred out for being too frustrating or overwhelming to continue treatment. Some psychotherapists, including Freud, found that initiating a psychotherapeutic alliance in the face of an intense transference (that was often acted out) was so problematic that it made Borderline Personality Disorder untreatable.[71] Before we get into treatment options,

---

69   A variety of sources discuss this, some of the earliest of which are Deutsch, H. (1942). Some forms of emotional disturbance and their relationship to schizophrenia. *Psychoanalytic Quarterly, 11*, 301–321.; Winnicott, D. W. (1965). *The maturational processes and the facilitating environment.* New York: International Universities Press.; and Kernberg, O. (1967). Borderline personality organization. *Journal of the American Psychoanalytic Association, 15*, 641–685.

70   Rinsley, D. B. (1976). *An object relations view of borderline personality.* Presented at the International Conference on Borderline Disorders, The Menninger Foundation and the National Institute of Mental Health, Topeka, Kansas, March 19–21, New York. The International Universities Press.

71   For discussion of the idea of borderline not being susceptible to treatment, see: Little, M. (1966). Transference in borderline states. *International Journal of Psycho-Analysis, 47*, 476–485.

let us consider a few questions, such as What is a borderline personality, and what are the symptomatic markers of the condition?[72] How did a borderline personality get to be that way? What are the secrets of successful treatment for this diagnostic category? In this chapter, we will address each of these subjects.

DSM-IV-TR (p. 710) identifies nine major characteristics of the borderline personality; a cluster of five characteristics is sufficient for diagnosis. Below is a summary of the DSM criteria.

1. Frantic efforts to avoid real or imagined abandonment.

2. A pattern of unstable and intense interpersonal relationships characterized by alternating between extremes of idealization and devaluation.

3. Identity disturbance: markedly and persistently unstable self-image or sense of self.

4. Impulsivity in at least areas that are potentially self-damaging.

5. Recurrent suicidal behavior, gestures, or threats, of self-mutilating behavior.

6. Affective instability resulting from a marked reactivity of mood.

7. Chronic feelings of emptiness.

8. Inappropriate, intense anger or difficulty controlling anger.

9. Transient, stress-related paranoid ideation or severe dissociative symptoms.

Some theorists talk about a stable personality organization that includes such symptoms as physical anxiety, polysymptomatic neurosis, polymorphous perverse sexual trends, pre-psychotic personality structures, impulsiveness/addictions, and character disorders.[73] It should be emphasized that there is a large difference between the concept of a personality organization and a personality disorder. Some experts have protested Kernberg's attempt to demarcate the two.[74]

Other practitioners have noted the following facets of Borderline Personality Disorders: splitting, autonomy conflicts, chaotic relationships, "stormy transferences,"

72   Some therapists still question whether Borderline Personality Disorder is a useful diagnosis: see Fromm, M. G. (1995). What does borderline mean? *Psychoanalytic Psychology, 12*(2), 233–245.; and Valliant, G. (1992). The beginning of wisdom is never calling a patient a borderline. *Journal of Psychotherapy Practice and Research, 1*, 117–134. We find these arguments unconvincing, however.
      Not only did DSM-IV-TR find sufficient justification in the research for a group of distinguishable symptomatologies to be described as Borderline Personality Disorder, but the vast amount of research on the subject by other clinicians supports it as well, including Gunderson's studies on whether or not there is a discriminable group of characteristics that might usefully be called borderline, which seems to yield definitive information. See two examples: Gunderson, J. G. (1978). Discriminating features of borderline patients. *American Journal of Psychiatry, 135*(7), 792–796.; and Gunderson, J. G. (1987). Current overview of the borderline diagnosis. Symposium: The Borderline Patient (1987, Boston, Massachusetts). *Journal of Clinical Psychiatry. 48*(Supplementary), 5–11.

73   For two classical examples of description of the borderline personality, see Kernberg, Ibid., and Gunderson, J. G. & Kolb, J. E. (1978). *American Journal of Psychiatry, 135*(7), 792–796.

74   Robbins, M. D. (1976). Borderline personality organization: The need for a new theory. *Journal of the American Psychoanalytic Association, 24*, 831–854.

negative counter-transferences, concreteness, attention-seeking, manipulativeness, somatization, inability to care for the self on a regular basis, occasional psychotic symptomatology, high oral needs, strong reactions to separations or felt abandonment, and problems with boundaries.[75] Recent research has found that a preponderance of malevolent or bad object relationships separates a borderline disorder from both healthier and more profoundly disturbed diagnostic categories.[76] Limited support also exists for the idea that patients diagnosed with Borderline Personality Disorder use transitional objects more often than in other diagnostic categories, as would be predicted from our theory.[77]

Almost any psychotherapist who has attempted to provide psychotherapy for Borderline Personality Disorder can quickly identify symptoms from the above list and relate "war stories" about the difficulties encountered, much as in Scenario 3 in Chapter 1, about Josh and Dr. Brown (note the intense fear of abandonment and his difficulties with boundaries). Often, the stories are sad, ending in one type of failure or another, recounted wistfully by a clinician who consciously wished for success but encountered failure. Failures are due in part to blinders on the clinician caused by his or her own typical repressions (such as disliking the patient or feeling burdened by them) and intense reactions (at least for this diagnostic category). These reactions are not what many psychotherapists have been trained to think they *must* feel for the people they attempt to help professionally. (A self-help book for psychotherapists treating Borderline Personality Disorder has been written to illustrate some of the dilemmas they feel.[78])

---

75 Gunderson, J. G. & Kolb, J. E. (1978). Discriminating features of borderline patients. *American Journal of Psychiatry, 135*, 792–796.

76 This determination is made using the earliest memory technique in: Nigg, J. T., Lohr, N. E., Westen, D., Gold, L. J., & Silk, K. R. (1992). Malevolent object relationships in borderline personality disorder and major depression. *Journal of Abnormal Psychology, 101*(1), 61–67. Also note: Arnow, D. & Harrison, R. H. (1991). Affect in early memories of borderline patients. *Journal of Personality Assessment, 56*(1), 75–83. These internal representations of the object as dangerous can be quite rigid and lead to negative transference reactions, a concept originally noticed by Freud, but later developed and expanded by Asch, Kernberg, Seinfeld, Valentine and others. (For a thorough discussion, see: Mordecai, E. M. (1995). Negative therapeutic reactions: Developing a new stance. *Psychoanalytic Psychology, 12*(4), 483–493.) Transference and counter-transference implications will be examined at length in Chapter 15.

77 A transitional object is a physical object that a young child might use in the absence of her soothing caregiver object. The most famous example of this today is Linus's use of the blanket in the cartoon strip "Peanuts" by Charles Schultz. Winnicott first described and developed the concept, noting that it particularly occurred in very young children (six months to three years) as they moved from a world they probably experienced as magical to one that was more reality-based. See Winnicott, D. W. (1958). Transitional objects and transitional phenomena. In *Collected papers: Through paediatrics to psycho-analysis* (pp. 229–242). London: Tavistock. (Original work published in 1951). One example of research support is in the article: Morris, H., Gunderson, J. G., & Zanarini, M. C. (1986). Transitional object use and borderline psychopathology. 137th Annual Meeting of the American Psychiatric Association (1984, Los Angeles, California). *American Journal of Psychiatry, 143*(12), 1534–1538.

78 Kreisman, J. J. & Straus, H. (1989). *I hate you—Don't leave me: Understanding the borderline personality.* New York: Avon.

We should make it clear that we are espousing a system of psychopathology that is based (for pre-Oedipal development) on the findings of Margaret Mahler and Otto Kernberg, two prominent figures in the American Object-Relations community (as distinct from the British Object Relations School, which includes Klein and Winnicott). The theory we propose, however, diverges from Kernberg's theory at several points, perhaps most significantly when discussing the developmental stage, in which the deficit that later results in a borderline personality occurred. Whether Kernberg's citation of Mahler[79] is a case of his listening to one suggestion she made and taking it too far, it seems to us that rather compelling evidence suggests that borderline syndrome is well associated with Mahler's hatching stage.[80]

All reasons for supporting this association center on the type of near-fused (associated with psychotic) development that is found in the borderline personality. Children who have successfully developed to the stage of rapprochement have developed a stable sense of differentiation or separateness in the previous stage of normal narcissism. This is not true of Borderline Personality Disorder, in which identity shifts, merges, and is not cohesive. Furthermore, the rapprochement child is secure as a separate person— he or she has gone through the practicing stage and does not feel overpowered when reapproaching his or her significant other, which is, again, not true of the borderline. People with Borderline Personality Disorder frequently attempt autonomy before they are truly ready for it, like the hatching-stage child. Especially during the late rapprochement stage, splitting is not a primary defense, but is entered into as a regression because of trauma.[81] In fact, rapprochement children, as a prerequisite for reapproaching the mother, must, in some way, be able to conceive of the "good" mother integrated with the "bad" mother (and "good" self with "the bad self"). To reapproach a part-object would

---

79   Kernberg, O. (1975). *Borderline conditions and pathological narcissism.* New York: Jason Aronson, Inc. ("These mechanisms, coercion and splitting of the object world, are characteristic in most cases of borderline transference" (pp. 155–156).)

80   Of course, if one takes the position that Kernberg does—that all character disorders from schizoid to narcissistic to depressive are actually borderline disorders—the discrimination between hatching and rapprochement stages becomes a bit more difficult. See Kernberg (1967, 1975) Ibid.

81   See an earlier footnote in which Kernberg quotes Mahler and note the quotes specifically about a *regression* during rapprochement causing the splitting. Note also the following quotations (and our editorial comments as marked) from Mahler, M. (1972). Rapprochement subphase of the separation-individuation process. *Psychoanalytic Quarterly, 41,* 487–506: "We have observed that children who achieve premature locomotor development, and are therefore able and prompted to separate physically from their mothers, may become prematurely aware of their own separateness much before their individuation (reality testing, cognition, etc.) has given them the means to cope with this awareness." Mahler clearly seems to be implying here, as she says two paragraphs later, that, normally, the differentiated child who comes out of the practicing stage is able to do reality testing and use his cognitive apparatus to considerable degree (as we might expect) and so has gone beyond rudimentary sensorimotor experiencing as she says two paragraphs later.

not be rapprochement at all.[82] Finally, it seems an axiom that people with a particular diagnosis have many traits from the stages that occur immediately before and after the stage in development at which they are "stuck," but not so many from developmental stages that are further away. Consequently, it makes the most sense to think of Borderline Personality Disorder, which has *many* psychotic traits and narcissistic features, to have a deficit or arrest that is in keeping with the stage *between* those related to psychosis or pathological narcissism—the hatching stage. Disorders relating to the rapprochement stage, which typically have features of narcissism and of the higher-order functioning of the neurotic (and not psychotic), as one would expect developmentally, are probably more like the near-neurotic self-system of the bipolar patient. This discussion will be presented later in more detail.

Getting back to the main discussion of Borderline Personality Disorder, and looking at Mahler's Stage 4 (hatching), in which the infant begins to break away from the caregiver and take initial steps toward independence, we can glean many clues as to the nature of the problems with borderline personality. This is not to say that people with Borderline Personality Disorder are simply "trapped" in Stage 4 of our developmental model; a more accurate image would be to say that the deanimated frozen wall indicating premature separation without sufficient maturity has encapsulated a personality structure similar to the child in the hatching stage.

First, and in particular, patients with borderline personalities are beset with a conflict about autonomy. Enough physical and psychological development has occurred to allow initial strivings toward independence, but, as in the child of this stage, their efforts must be limited, with frequent checking back to a caregiver who really "holds it together" for them. Psychotherapists frequently tell stories of patients who come in one week with a life-and-death struggle and who, the following week, feel ready to terminate psychotherapy and try independence on their own. The experienced psychotherapist, like the good parent,

---

Mahler also states: "On the other hand, we have found that in infants with overprotective and infantilizing mothers, individuation may develop well ahead, and may result in a lag of boundary formation and a lag in readiness to function as a separate individual without undue anxiety." This latter group of infants she describes, who do not quite complete the process of differentiation (do not successfully complete the stage of normal narcissism), sound much more like those with borderline personality. Also take note of this quotation, from the same article: "We believe that it is during this rapprochement subphase that the foundation for subsequent 'normal neurotic,' or neurosis with borderline features, is set." She does not say anything suggestive of a borderline diagnosis but, to the contrary, talks of children who successfully transverse this subphase as being normal or neurotic or of having borderline *features*. Features are not the same as a borderline personality organization or disorder.

82   In Chapter 9, on stable or characterological depressions, extensive discussion is provided on the initial steps to regard self and others as whole, which we believe is intrinsic to rapprochement. We do not argue, nor does Mahler, that the initial steps toward experiencing other and self as whole are neutralized or complex, but we will save further comment on these developments until the appropriate time.

must not allow this. The psychotherapist may forestall the termination with a perspective that reminds the patient of the desperate struggle with which they were dealing only a short time ago. At the same time, the psychotherapist should compliment the patient on his or her progress and greater strength. Sometimes, when his or her perspective is not convincing enough, the skillful psychotherapist makes a temporary compromise (such as putting the next appointment off an extra week in recognition of the newly gained strength). Meanwhile, the psychotherapist continues to provide a therapeutic holding structure that the patient can continue to depend on. Quite often, these compromises are in word only, as the patient with Borderline Personality Disorder, needing help, calls in with another crisis before the next appointment occurs.

Second, patients with borderline personalities are only centimeters away (developmentally) from the symbiotic selfobject stage in which they only dimly recognized their own needs, feelings, and selves through the empathic response of the caregiver. One result of this developmental proximity is the maturational propulsion away from engulfment by the caregiver, which must be respected. Just as quickly, however, the patients feel their incapacity to function on their own and snap back into the wish for a merger with the psychotherapist to manage affairs that have quickly become unmanageable. A treating mental health professional who does not understand this conflict quite often becomes frustrated and confused and is tempted to push patients away far too soon for their capacities to cope.

Third, like children at this stage of development, people with Borderline Personality Disorder are beset with massive amalgams of feelings of pleasure or pain arranged around whether or not gratification has taken place. Lacking the independent ego mastery to integrate or neutralize these feelings, the borderline personality "splits" both self and object into gratifying (good) and frustrating (bad) parts—the borderline personality can have wholesale negative reactions to the self (leading to suicidal actions or self-mutilations) as well as complete rejections of an unrecognized caring psychotherapist or of anyone else who is seen as frustrating. The psychotherapist, like the good parent at this stage of development, must help the patient to neutralize and integrate split-off, disavowed self- and object representations and the intense, primitive affects associated with them. The stance of being the "calm, stable object" is good basic advice, for it allows the patient to use the psychotherapist as a managing "alter ego" and to organize him- or herself around the psychotherapist's wholeness and stability.

It should also be noted that the splitting described in the previous paragraph is not restricted to the internal world of the patient; instead, the person who gratifies is treated as an all-good, idealized object, while the person who limits or deprives is often treated as the all-bad, devalued object. The treatment that the patient metes out to average citizens or members of a treatment team such as might be found on an inpatient unit can be devastating to those who lack insight into the patient's condition. What happens is that those who are treated well will, like the person with borderline personality, feel sorry for the patient's plight and encourage nurturance, while the person treated as the bad object will resent the treatment, find the patient uncooperative and ungrateful and will wish to further manage the patient with more limitations. On many occasions, in a hospital milieu or in everyday life, this will mean that the "good" and the "bad" objects (people) will come into conflict about how the patient should be treated, and the staff or social support system will become "split" as well. Such splits must be healed if the borderline is to improve, but can only be overcome with proper insight into what is happening. Healing the split in the social system holding the person with a borderline personality can lead to unification of splits within the borderline personality.

Fourth, the borderline personality is like the child just coming out of symbiosis who understands himself poorly and is highly dependent on the caregiver's ability to correctly "mind-read" the needs of the patient. The psychotherapist must, at this point, direct or manage the patient into gratifying, or at least neutral, behaviors.

Fifth, like the symbiotic or hatching child, the borderline personality has not yet achieved a stable, well-differentiated self. Instead, he or she is possessed of a fragmentary, poorly integrated self reminiscent of Stage 2 development—a self that is held together only by the good empathic management of the caregiver. One result of this is the presence of symptoms typical of self-organization that is fragmentary and barely held together, particularly when stress is present.

Sixth, anxiety in the patient with Borderline Personality Disorder is manifested as it is in children (not verbally, but in the form of physical tension) because of the many unintegrated, conflicted parts of the self. Again, only an understanding, calm, stable caregiver can help the borderline ease the edges of this strong anxiety and take effective action toward pulling together the different aims of the parts of the disintegrated self.

Seventh, people with Borderline Personality Disorder feel empty, as they have internalized the caregiving ego strategies of the caregiver to only a marginal degree.[83] A physical deficit occurring at this developmental period can be met only by the management

---

83 See a discussion of this in Arnow & Harrison, Ibid. Another study that provides research support and further shows the relationship between faulty Object-Relations and thought disturbance is Berg, J. L., Packer, A., & Nunno, V .J. (1993). A Rorschach analysis: Parallel disturbance in thought and self/object representation. *Journal of Personality Assessment, 61*(2), 311–323.

of an integrated, understanding person in charge, such as a good parent or a wise psychotherapist. Strong negative reactions to separations, strangers, and felt abandonment, as would be typical of the Stage 4 child in our developmental model, would be typical.

Eighth, the borderline personality is only a step away from the stages that in our theory are associated with psychosis and the lack of consensually understood boundaries. Consequently, periods of psychotic-like behavior can occur. Intense stranger anxiety, probably better called paranoia, may result. Loss of boundaries regarding who has caused what may occur, which leads to transferences in which the psychotherapist, in the patient's view, can be held entirely responsible for the patient's discomfort. This transference may take place in spite of actions the patient may have engaged in to cause the dilemma. Hallucinations, perhaps best understood as regressive to the organization of Stage 2, can also result.

Counter-transference Reactions and Therapeutic Techniques

The average person is ill-equipped to handle the pushes and pulls of the adult with Borderline Personality Disorder. The average person might be able to manage the strong variations in the mood of a child, guide that "ignorant" child toward gratification that the child only dimly understands, and help such a child learn about the boundaries of the adult world, but the average person with whom a patient with Bipolar Personality Disorder interacts will experience her as a difficult, unreasonable, and sometimes dramatic, dangerous, or explosive individual.

Because psychotherapists are also average people, they, too, are pulled by these same forces and may develop a strong distaste for the pushing and pulling of patients with Bipolar Personality Disorder. A typical scenario might involve the patient failing an afternoon appointment (because she was caught up in something else, was feeling strong enough to cope with life on her own, or had some other reason, such as Josh in Scenario 3 of Chapter 1) and then showing up at another time for an unscheduled appointment, usually at some other patient's time. The patient may even make a desperate crisis-call later during the day or do something self-destructive without contacting the psychotherapist. Needless to say, these kinds of pushes and pulls can be extremely taxing and irritating, especially if the psychotherapist has no way of understanding what the patient is going through.

Related to the abandonment and boundary issues that are ever-present for him or her, the person with borderline personality is struggling to establish a sense of object constancy, as stated in earlier discussion of Mahler's Developmental Theory, related to the failure of internalizing the soothing functions of significant others, such as the caregiver. It is like the hatching-age child who seems delighted, over and over, with the game of peek-a-boo as he finds that the caregiving object has not simply disappeared because he can't momentarily see or hear her. We have had many patients tell us (and other psychotherapists confirm it with stories from their own patients) that they call our answering service or answering machine, play our tapes, or anything to simply remind themselves that we still exist. Eventually, our presence, if it is useful enough, is internalized, and the patient does not suffer senses of abandonment as before.[84]

With a proper understanding, the psychotherapist is unruffled by such behavior, as he or she understands the dynamics. He or she is also calm in the face of demands to merge lives (like the patient trying to intrude on the private life of the psychotherapist), much like the good parent would be unruffled by the child of Stage 4 opening the bathroom door and walking in unannounced. Unspoken, yet strong demands to "read my mind and tell me what is wrong and what to do" would be met in a similar calm way, much like the parent would expect to do with a child of 9 to 30 months.

A useful rule of thumb for the psychotherapist treating a borderline is not *pure* indulgence (this usually leads first to feeling like a hero and then to feeling overwhelmed and finally to rejection of the patient as the heroic efforts fails). Instead, the psychotherapist must walk a fine line between gratifying certain needs of the borderline (while respecting his or her own needs)[85] and limiting or redirecting the efforts of the borderline toward productive behavior. Because the ego or coping mechanisms of the borderline are so weak and the borderline is not struggling primarily with strong, well-formed parts of the self in conflict with one another, like the more developed neurotic, the psychotherapist does not, generally, attempt to practice a more classical psychoanalysis. It is essential that the psychotherapist be informed of the psychodynamics of the patient, but, like dealing with a child, *act* on these understandings in the relationship with direction, limit-setting, and management. Much like the parent who might say to the young child, "I'm feeding you now because you are hungry," the psychotherapist might verbalize some of what they are doing in a teaching way; the psychotherapist does not count, however, on such verbalizations as a cure, but only as information provided for learning for the patient.

There has been some criticism of the use of the relationship rather than timely, correct interpretations of conflict as a curative technique (the more classical analytic

---

84   A good discussion of this idea can be found in Volkan, V. D. (1994). Identification with the therapist's functions and ego-building in the treatment of schizophrenia. *British Journal of Psychiatry, 164*(23), 77–82.

85   Here, we must agree with the comments of Kernberg about "supportive psychotherapy" for the borderline personality, at least in part, although we believe he does not properly understand Masterson and the others who espouse that concept (Kernberg, 1967, 1975, Ibid.). See also Masterson, J. F. (1990). Psychotherapy of borderline and narcissistic disorders: Establishing a therapeutic alliance (a developmental, self and object relations approach). *Journal of Personality Disorders, 4*(2), 182–191.

approach).[86] Although we have some sympathy with an apparent attempt by some practitioners (perhaps out of ignorance to the huge Freudian legacy, as suggested by Busch, referenced in the previous footnote, or perhaps for some other reason) to reduce all people's problems to pre-Oedipal deficits that left their self-structures fragile, we cannot fathom giving a two- or three-year-old a rational explanation and expecting them to understand and follow it. We have had no more luck using a rational or cognitive approach with Borderline Personality Disorder, for, as Kernberg and others point out, patients are incredibly concrete, even childlike, in their understandings of things, *almost as if the use of their cognitive apparatus has been arrested,* either at the sensorimotor or in Piaget's concrete operational stages. The arrest could be due to trauma or developmental deficits but leaves the person with borderline personality with symptoms typical of the childhood ages our deficit[87] theory is postulating.

As a final word on transference, counter-transference, and the use of the relationship in the cure, the *compelling* nature of the transference, which is largely nonverbal and acted out as if it were currently true and the psychotherapist were one of the original perpetrators of frustration, can be experienced as a measure of the types of drives and the level of organization typical of a childhood stage of development.[88] If the borderline personality can truly be related to the largely nonverbal toddler, one might begin to understand how a psychotherapist might feel if his patient, a toddler with adult size and abilities, were to meander off into the middle of a busy highway, or alternatively, bite and throw a tantrum because he did not get his way on some issue. Some transferences certainly *can* be profitably analyzed with intelligent reason and discussed with words, in certain patients and at certain times. The transferences of the borderline personality are not spoken, however; instead, the psychotherapist finds himself, without a word being spoken, as a player in a role he did not choose. These latter transferences provoke incredibly strong and useful reactions or counter-transferences in the psychotherapist and are best primarily handled,

---

86   Murray, J. F., Ibid.; Busch, F. (1995). Resistance analysis and Object Relations Theory: Erroneous conceptions amidst some timely contributions. *Psychoanalytic Psychology, 12*(1), 43–53.

87   One of the major differences between Object-Relations Theory and Self-Psychology, as juxtaposed against classical Psychoanalysis, is that the former two put more emphasis on *deficits*, while the latter puts more emphasis on *conflicts* between parts of the self. We believe there is a place for both ideas and will more fully treat the difference just described in Chapter 16. It should also be mentioned that all the above theories have equal regard for the concept of developmental arrest.

88   An early classical article that describes this phenomenon is Rosenfeld, H. (1978). Notes on the psychopathology and psychoanalytic treatment of some borderline patients. *International Journal of Psycho-Analysis, 59*, 215–221. See also Summers, Ibid. and Kernberg (1975). Ibid. For the even more serious student, a comprehensive treatment of the "new" understanding of counter-transference is presented in an excellent way in Tansey, M. J. & Burke, W. (1989). *Understanding countertransference: From projective identification to empathy.* New York: The Analytic Press.

as they are presented, nonverbally in the relationship. The psychotherapist is treated as a frustrating object but must act with the wisdom of the good parent of a child at this age.

Early psychoanalysts (and even some contemporary ones) say that character disorders such as Borderline Personality Disorder are untreatable using the psychoanalytic method. Some modern psychoanalysts will say a modification of technique, called psychoanalytic psychotherapy, which has the psychotherapist taking a much more active, face-to-face role (described above) makes the condition treatable.

According to our theory, the borderline personality has a stable but pathologically arrested development and so is difficult to treat. Some experts, after an examination of statistics, state that the average patient with borderline personality will be hospitalized several times (for short stabilization stays; longer stays, though rare these days, require less frequency) during their recovery.[89] Anecdotal evidence from psychotherapists supports a therapeutic approach of balancing attention between helping and allowing independence in the treatment of the borderline patient. Considering the constraints imposed by managed care, a balanced outpatient treatment is preferable to multiple hospitalizations for stabilization, containment of dangerous behavior directed at self or others, or consultation. One clinician we know who has treated many patients with Borderline Personality Disorder alleges that the average number of short-term hospitalizations (which he is treating primarily with outpatient care) is six, according to his records. Regardless of the number of short-term hospitalizations we can expect, outpatient psychotherapists, using a brief psychotherapy orientation, with hospitalization being used only for containment and stabilization, need to be told about this so that when their patients come up for multiple hospitalizations, they will not feel like failures. Inpatient treatment staff need to be made aware of this for the same reason. Long-term hospitalizations inevitably lead to regression, even to psychotic proportions, and can be undertaken only if the resources are truly

---

89   See especially Snyder, S., Pitts, W. M., & Pokorny, A. D. (1986). Selected behavioral features of patients with borderline personality traits. *Suicide and Life-Threatening Behavior, 16*(1), 28–39.
      The following articles also are worth reviewing, as they discuss the issues well, but *take careful note of the length of the hospital stays they are discussing, for, in most cases, it is what we would today call long-term intensive treatment:* Marcus, E. (1987). Relationship of illness and intensive hospital treatment to length of stay. *Psychiatric Clinics of North America, 10*(2), 247–255.; Marcus, E. & Bradley, S. (1987). Concurrence of Axis I and Axis II illness in treatment-resistant hospitalized patients. *Psychiatric Clinics of North America, 10*(2), 177–184.; Rosenbluth, M. (1987). The inpatient treatment of the borderline personality disorder: A critical review and discussion of aftercare implications. *Canadian Journal of Psychiatry, 32,* 228–237.; Stone, M. H., Stone, D. K., & Hurt, S. W. (1987). Natural history of borderline patients treated by intensive hospitalization. *Psychiatric Clinics of North America, 10*(2), 185–206.
      For a discussion of the differences in approach and expectation when either short- or long-term treatment of Borderline Personality Disorder is attempted, also see Gordon, C. & Beresin, E. (1983). Conflicting treatment models for the inpatient management of borderline patients. *American Journal of Psychiatry, 140*(8), 979–983.

available or if the patient's environmental resources are so limited that to return to the environment would lead to further decompensation. As mentioned above, however, good long-term inpatient treatment has been shown to produce a variety of positive outcomes and to drastically reduce recidivism, often requiring only one hospitalization[90] (although the total number of days in the hospital may still be greater than for other conditions).

Long-term hospitalization is a rarity these days. Most patients with borderline personality, like other patients, are treated on an outpatient basis. As a recent outcome study showed, this outpatient treatment will require many sessions to reach an "effective dose."[91] Still, a capable, knowledgeable, empathic, stable, and calm psychotherapist can help the patient learn enough about herself to produce more effective coping techniques. The psychotherapist can help the patient neutralize otherwise massive affect so that the patient may progress to the point where she is truly able to function for long periods of time with little interference. The psychotherapist will still need to take an appreciative and protective stance, treating the patient defensively stuck at the next developmental stage (narcissism).

Before concluding, one final comment needs to be made concerning the typical fears and defenses of the patient with Borderline Personality Disorder. Fears of abandonment, domination, and annihilation are common. Defensive operations (many of which have already been discussed) include primitive idealization, projective identification, denial, omnipotence, devaluation, chaos, dependency to the point of fusion and splitting. Again, even a quick glance at these fears and defenses tells us that we are dealing with different symptoms than the more neurotic or usual patients that pass through our doors. The psychotherapist who is aware of this will be prepared with a combination of management skills. The psychotherapist will need very concrete interpretations, often coupled with direction, and a sense of perspective and stability like a good parent would use with a small child; he will need to gather all this around a core of calmness to help the patient incorporate new internalized object-relations (through the psychotherapist) that will fill in the holes and correct the mistakes of the previous self-structure.

The host of symptoms found in Borderline Personality Disorder can be understood and effectively treated using the same model. Some symptoms, such as addictions, may need to be addressed and treated concurrently using methods specifically effective for those conditions. No two borderline personalities are alike, so each treatment plan must be unique, but the basics for all treatment plans flow from a group of the same model and dynamics.

---

90   See references previously footnoted for documentation.
91   Kopta, S. M., Howard, K. I., Lowry, J. L., & Beutler, L. E. (1994). Patterns of symptomatic recovery in psychotherapy. *Journal of Consulting and Clinical Psychology, 62*(5), 1009–1016. Also see Seligman, M. (1995). Mental health: Does therapy help? *Consumer Reports, November,* 734–739.

CHAPTER 9

PATHOLOGICAL NARCISSISM: PEOPLE WHOM NO ONE LIKES

O ver the past few years, we have been listening to our colleagues as they discuss people for whom they are considering, or have already given, the diagnosis of Narcissistic Personality Disorder. Though our report is only a clinical anecdote, what we have observed is that many of these clinicians cannot seem to talk about narcissistic personality without a curl on their upper lips, indicating disdain or even scorn. We have even come to believe that, sometimes, clinicians get angry at their patients and toss the narcissistic diagnosis around, almost as if they were getting revenge.

Narcissism is as old as the ancient Greek story of Narcissus; the concept, however, was given new life by Freud and has become central to our thinking in psychotherapy. This is especially true since the advent of Self-Psychology, though Object-Relations Theory and Integrative Theory also have helped to make the concept popular.

The authors' belief is that the negativity associated with the concept of narcissism is also associated and confused with healthy narcissism. This stems from two sources. The critical understanding of both the association and confusion between these facets of narcissism may be instructive as well as useful to the psychotherapist in working with a patient with deep narcissistic injuries or even possessing a Narcissistic Personality Disorder. First, we believe that consideration of narcissism continues to be tainted by 19th-century moralism, which equates it with selfishness, a quality deemed bad in many societies.[92] Second, people with narcissistic personality stir up our own conflicts with

---

92   We attribute this to a faulty understanding of religious tenets, such as that which may lead people to elevate "Love

narcissism, either through adoring us or through ignoring us (and many other forms of treatment between those extremes). Our own narcissism may therefore be inflated, which can threaten the self-structure we have developed over the years. This is particularly true if we have come to regard ourselves as unselfish (by trampling on our own self-esteem) or have seen these narcissistic features and qualities as good. In most people, expressing a love of self will produce a knee-jerk defensive reaction.

To complicate matters further, numerous definitions of narcissism exist. Three of the most prominent are Freud's (in his discussion of primary and pathological narcissism[93]), Theodore Millon's (in his book *Modern Psychopathology*[94] and in the psychological instruments in widespread use based on Millon's theories), and that of the Self- and Object-Relations psychologists. DSM-IV-TR's definition is not absolute to any particular psychological theory, so its description of Narcissistic Personality Disorder must not be confused or identified only with the narcissism described in neo-analytic thinking. Finally, there are those psychotherapists within the fields of Self-Psychology and Object-Relations Theory who discuss the possibility that a Narcissistic Personality Disorder may just be a better-developed borderline personality organization (Kernberg, however, thinks it may be a less-developed borderline organization).[95]

In the presentation of our model of the mind (as used in this book), we will disagree with Freud's and some of his followers' thinking, in that we don't believe that an infant is born into a state of primary narcissism.[96] As you may remember from earlier chapters, it seems more accurate to state that the child is born into a state of streaming, confused consciousness, with some in-built structures that predispose the infant to bonding. In Mahler's developmental model, the fundamental building block of the pre-Oedipal

---

thy neighbor" instead of the dictum "Love thy neighbor *as thyself,*" which is the correct tradition (italics added for emphasis). For that reason, it may be beneficial to consider 19th-century philosopher Jeremy Bentham's concept of enlightened self-interest as an alternative to the fallacy of the popular understanding of narcissism.

93   Freud, S. (1957). On narcissism. *The standard edition of the complete psychological works of Sigmund Freud (Vol. 14).* London: Hogarth Press. (See especially pp. 73–102) Original work published 1914.

94   Millon, T. (1983). *Modern psychopathology: A biosocial approach to maladaptive learning and functioning.* New York: Waveland Press.

95   Kernberg, O. (1975). *Borderline conditions and pathological narcissism.* New York: Jason Aronson, Inc. (p. 18). See also an early work of Kohut & Wolf that describes a variety of patients with narcissism whom most practitioners today would describe as having borderline personalities (particularly those with "merger transferences" and the "fragmenting self"), although the authors say (p. 415) that the borderline diagnosis is different from the narcissistic: Kohut, H. & Wolf, E. S. (1978). The disorders of the self and their treatment: An outline. *International Journal of Psycho-Analysis, 59,* 413–425 (especially pages 418 and 422).

96   Although the following are secondary sources, they do make reference to the developmental placement of narcissism in Freud's thought and in the thought of those in Self-Psychology and Object-Relations. See: St. Clair, M. (2004). *Object relations and self psychology: An introduction* (2nd ed.). Pacific Grove, CA: Brooks/Cole (pp. 112–113 and 161–163). and Brenner, C. (1974). *An elementary textbook of psychoanalysis* (revised ed.). Garden City, NY: Anchor Books (pp. 98–99).

portion of the model of this book, narcissism is viewed as a *development*, not as an initial "given." We place it around Stage 5 of our developmental model and state that if pathology develops, it is as if a defensive wall of separation forms prematurely around this state of organization, before the child has the mastery skills to continue developing beyond the stage. Whether this is by deficit or trauma cannot be said for all cases. The evidence of narcissistic injury is often rampant, though we have found cases in which it simply seemed that the child was overindulged and not encouraged to grow up. It is clear, however, with the hypothesis of the premature separation and defensive wall around the narcissistic position, that, again, we are not talking about psychopathologizing normal development, but there appears to be much to learn about the functioning of the adult with Narcissistic Personality Disorder based on an understanding of our developmental Stage 5.

In Stage 5, the separation that began with physical locomotion in the previous hatching stage crystallizes into a self-structure that is hyperindividualized. (This is what is attempted to be shown by drawing the self with a solid line around it, but with the object representation having a dotted line around it, almost as if it doesn't exist.) As dependent as the young baby was, particularly through the symbiotic stage, the narcissist appears to be as independent. As discussed in Chapter 4, there is good reason, however, from observing children in this stage, to believe that hyperindividualism is more of an appearance than a reality, but the child does act as if no one else exists.[97] This is the time of "I, me, mine" and "I want." Observers comment on the child's imperviousness to hurts occurred on the way to obtaining the object that he or she is seeking,[98] as well as the apparent disregard for limit-setting attempts made by the parents. Some authors have said that this is a time when the world is the child's "oyster"[99] for him or her to explore, taste, and have. The mastery skills intrinsic to Mahler's view of individuation are practiced repeatedly in many variations until the child is confident enough in his or her abilities to cope in certain areas. Parents find material objects taken apart and evidence that a certain toddler was in an unexpected portion of the house sometime during the day.

The good parent's job during this time is to appreciate the efforts of the child (as unobtrusively as possible), protect the child from harm, and demonstrate solutions. The gleam in the parent's eye is the outward precursor to the child's development of self-

---

97   For a description of the apparent obliviousness, see Mahler, M. (1972). Rapprochement subphase of the Separation-Individuation Process. *Psychoanalytic Quarterly, 41*, 492–493.
         For thoughts about development and individuation, with an excellent description of a narcissistic reaction to a longed-for missing mother in a practicing-aged child (p. 321), see Mahler, M. (1963). Thoughts about development and individuation. *Psychoanalytic Study of the Child, 18*, 307–324.
98   Mahler, M. (1972). op. cit., p. 493.
99   Mahler, M. (1972). op. cit., p. 495.

esteem, as he and his efforts are first esteemed by his caregivers.[100] Because the child finds the world fascinating and cannot conceive of any limit to his ability, save that which is yet unlearned, he needs to be protected with limits. Finally, the child also will need to have someone to look up to, who helps him solve problems so he can internalize an admirable ego-ideal, which will again be an important part of his self-esteem.[101]

People with Narcissistic Personality Disorder also seem to relate to others along the lines of whether the other (object) is gratifying or frustrating. When an object is gratifying, it is a good object to be used.[102] When an object is limiting or frustrating, it is a bad object to be the target of aggression or to be ignored. At this stage of development, as in the previous stage, the child is still largely governed by the largeness of feeling good and gratified, or of feeling bad and frustrated, though she may have subcategories of feelings under these general reactions. Still, many have noted the child's complete demonstration of rage (red face, clenched fists, striking out to the person who is holding her, distended nostrils, showing teeth or gums, etc.) when she does not get what she wants. A shift to a complete state of bliss, without a visible crease in the forehead, with eventual cooing and smiling and lack of bodily tension, can be quickly produced if the child is given what she wants. Again, these shifts seem total, can happen quickly, and are fluid in the child (that is, the bad object of a few minutes before can become the good object of now, simply through gratification).[103]

The narcissistic stage of the child has just led to hatching out of the symbiotic egg and allows for the development of a separate identity. Is it any wonder that one of the chief fears of children at this stage seems to be that of being re-engulfed, dominated, or enveloped? Is it any wonder that these children—and the adults stuck at this level of development—seem to be shy of intimacy? In the deeper layers of their minds, closeness is threatening.[104]

Narcissistic Personality Disorder is noted for its apparent imperturbable and grandiose self-esteem[105] and feelings of entitlement. Some authors theorize that adult

---

100 Mahler, M. (1963). op. cit., pp. 317–318; Kohut & Wolf, op. cit., p. 417.
101 Kohut & Wolf, p. 417.
102 Kernberg, O. (1975). op. cit., pp. 272–273.
103 Obviously, this is almost identical to what was described in the last chapter and is probably one reason that Kernberg and others have talked about the "underlying borderline personality organization" of many narcissistic personalities. See Kernberg, O. (1975). op. cit., p. 15.
104 See footnote number 11.
105 In fact, one study found the criteria describing grandiosity as the most useful in discriminating narcissistic from borderline patients: Ronningstam, E. & Gunderson, J. G. (1991). Differentiating Borderline Personality Disorder from Narcissistic Personality Disorder. 142nd Annual Meeting of the American Psychiatric Association (1989, San Francisco, CA). *Journal of Personality Disorders*, 5(3), 225–232.
        See also: Little, T., Watson, P. J., Biderman, M. D., & Ozbek, I. N. (1992). Narcissism and object relations. *Psychological Reports*, 71, 799–808. Little, et al., again find support for the concept of the grandiose self in a large sample of college students who completed the Narcissistic Personality Inventory but did not find support for the idealizing component of Kohut's theory (which, of course, does not discredit this part of his theory but simply did not find support for the latter concept).

patients with Narcissistic Personality Disorder have continued the state of symbiotic bliss or well-being into the smaller container of their individual self-boundaries.[106] Others note that this self-esteem is brittle and vulnerable to injury.[107] When the sense of the child's worth or entitlement is upset, the results are often experienced as devastating, presumably because internal coping structures and defenses are still in development and remain deficient. The child needs an alter ego to keep her equilibrium, like a separate version of the incorporated object in the self/object of the symbiotic state. Without this alter ego, the child can become depressed, sullen, angry, and vengeful. Similar reactions are noted in adults with Narcissistic Personality Disorder in the event of loss or separation from a significant other (who, interestingly enough, frequently reports feeling ignored and used). Perhaps Josh's girlfriend in the Scenario 3 of Chapter 1 felt this, and Dr. Brown was treating more of a narcissistic personality than a borderline personality.

The second major task needing completion during this stage is the development of an independent self-esteem. Previously, in the symbiotic stage (and even to some degree in the hatching stage), esteem was implicit in the value of, and the caregiving responses of, the object that was seen as part of the self at that time. Within the separation of narcissism, however, the child (or adult) seems to need a steady stream of "sunshine" (appreciation) from the caregiver to keep this sense of personal value going. Furthermore, the valuing from the other needs to be complete, with no major blind spots, or the child will develop feelings of being conditionally valued, with low self-esteem in other areas holding him back in those areas.

Typical Transferences

Kohut has done the most detailed job of defining the types of transferences likely to be noted in the adult with Narcissistic Personality Disorder.[108] The comparisons with children in the stage of normal narcissism are striking. He describes four types of transference, discussed below.

1. Merger transference is used primarily by low-functioning Narcissistic Personality Disorders, in which the psychotherapist is expected to more or less "move in and take control." This transference is most reminiscent of the symbiotic state.

---

106   For a brief discussion of this idea, see Kernberg, O. (1975). op. cit., pp. 275–276.
107   Kohut, H. (1972). Thoughts on narcissism and narcissistic rage. *The Psychoanalytic Study of the Child* (Vol. 27). New York: Quadrangle Books. In this article, Kohut uses the metaphor of the organic reaction in the brain-damaged patient, who senses he lacks the capability to respond to a threat and so throws whatever destructive means are available within himself, or at his fingertips, at the problem confronting him.
108   See Kohut & Wolf, Ibid.; and Kohut, H. (1984). *How does analysis cure?* Edited by Arnold Goldberg, in collaboration with Paul E. Stepansky. London: University of Chicago Press. (The last of Kohut's books, this work was published posthumously.)

2. Mirroring transference is used when the patient wants to "do his own thing" but be appreciated and understood. Being an almost constant object of attention is also considered important. Although the patient sees him- or herself as being separate from the clinician, the clinician is significant only to the extent of fulfilling the patient's needs for confirmation of his or her greatness, talent, etc.

3. Idealizing transference occurs much the same way that a child picks up a sense of stature, or lack thereof, through the process of association with his caregivers.[109] Here, the patient strives to remain in a state of togetherness with the clinician, who is experienced as an "ideal image" of perfection and greatness—which can be conferred upon the patient via association to the object.

4. Alter ego and twinship transferences also are mentioned but are considered less important and common. They are just as their name suggests: intermediate to the main three transferences. That is, they are more attenuated versions of the others. The psychotherapist is experienced as being "like" the patient.

Counter-transference Reactions and Therapeutic Techniques

When we speak of counter-transference here, we do so in the more encompassing way first made popular by Winnicott[110] and recently described in careful detail in books by Tansey and Burke and by Summers.[111] The basic idea is that people with the character disorders—narcissism included—"suck out" of the people with whom they come into contact, feeling[112] reactions that are complementary to their own and thus maintain a sort of miserable pathological homeostasis to their life conditions.[113]

Because of self-esteem vulnerabilities, people with Narcissistic Personality Disorder frequently will go to great lengths to demonstrate their worth (wearing gold Rolex watches and fine clothing, scorning others, dropping names, etc.), all of which strike most people as being grandiose and/or offensive to their own self-esteem. The average person, and

---

109   Klein, M. (1975). *Envy and gratitude and other works, 1946–1963*. New York: Delta Books (See pp. 25–42, "On the theory of anxiety and guilt"). Original work published in 1948. Also see Schafer, R. (1968). *Aspects of internalization*. New York: International Universities Press.

110   Winnicott, D. W. (1949). Hate in the counter-transference. *The International Journal of Psych-Analysis, 30*(2), 69–74.

111   Tansey, M. J., & Burke, W. F. (1989). *Understanding counter-transference: From projective identification to empathy*. Hillsdale, NJ: The Analytic Press. Also see Summers, F. (1994). *Object relations theory and psychopathology: A comprehensive text*. Hillsdale, NJ: The Analytic Press.

112   The word "feeling" may not be adequate here because the person on the other end, who is experiencing the type of counter-transference a character-disordered person can stir up, virtually *finds* himself in a role, complete with expected actions, thoughts, behaviors, and feelings.

113   Kernberg, O. (1975). op. cit, pp. 275–276.

even psychotherapists, will be sorely tempted to counterattack with depreciation or with similar demonstrations of worth. Some experts even counsel confrontation of the narcissist for well-reasoned explanations, but we have rarely seen confrontation work well.[114] Reactions like these are unfortunate for the patient, for they strike at the heart of what the patient is trying to accomplish in a childish way: a sense of appreciated worth.

According to our theory, for a narcissistic personality to graduate to the next stage of development, she must understand the nuances of her feelings, find adequate coping mechanisms to become more balanced and neutral, and be able to cope. Such understanding comes largely from the experience of being understood. It is a hallmark of the narcissistic child to wish to do the talking and be understood, not vice versa, and not even in a shared fashion. Previous generations of parents have found this quite frustrating and have tried to "beat" some concern for others into the child (which has disastrous consequences); however, if the parent or, later, the psychotherapist can offer focused understanding (sometimes even needing to be unspoken, lest the narcissist feel interrupted, as illustrated in Scenario 2 of Chapter 1 with Sue and Dr. Stone), the person eventually can learn enough about herself to move on to interest in others. If she is provided nonintrusive empathy, she will feel secure enough about being independent that she might even risk approaching others again, because her concerns about engulfment will be lessened. Supplying such an unbroken supply of empathy, with little coming back, is either very draining or tedious for a psychotherapist, however. Although extensive and extended periods of management may be necessary, with an often unreflective and even contentious patient, consistent, patient, quiet (metaphorical) holding of the treatment situation and patient until she is able to hear and truly engage is the essence of any treatment that is psychoanalytic. Psychotherapists can get frustrated, lose track of what the patient is saying, or simply feel sucked dry. Special training can help with this, as can the understanding and use of our theory to micromanage the relationship, watching for otherwise-unnoticed minuscule steps toward integration.

Because the person with Narcissistic Personality Disorder has only two basic emotional states, he may regard the psychotherapist as a bad object if the psychotherapist

---

114   Kernberg, O. (1978). pp. 263–314. Kernberg says that a more supportive approach (than with borderline personality?) generally works best with these patients (p. 249); however, his approach is far less supportive than that suggested by Kohut and his followers, who seek to make the patient's experience as "near" as possible to the therapist.
     See: Basch, M. 1988). *Understanding psychotherapy.* New York: Basic Books (pp. 129–153). Perhaps this is why Kernberg, and not Kohut, paints a rather dismal prognostic picture for the patient with Narcissistic Personality Disorder. (See: Kernberg, Ibid., p. 48.)

is seen as frustrating rather than gratifying. This can lead to projective identification[115] or other negative transference reactions.[116] Because the narcissistic personality is more structurally developed than the borderline personality, the slippage between emotional states is less, so the problem becomes greater for the psychotherapist. If the psychotherapist is seen by a narcissistic personality as a bad object, he must immediately retreat into the most basic mirroring and supportive positions until the patient's trust is regained. The psychotherapist must then be returned to the status of a gratifying object before any analysis of the therapeutic break can be attempted.

Narcissistic Rage

Much has been made of the narcissist's penchant for rage, revenge, and vendettas.[117] In our clinical experience, this happens only with more severe Narcissistic Personality Disorder. The best two ways to explain reactions like these are contained in a classical paper by Kohut, in which he compares the reactions to the catastrophic reaction of the organic patient, who flies out with all the fury available in an unfocused reaction because he lacks the internal resources to direct himself into more-focused problem-solving behavior.[118] The second example Kohut gives could be called the unhealed-wound metaphor, in which the other has either intentionally, or more likely unintentionally, touched the open sore where self-esteem is at its weakest. Here again, the narcissistic personality is likely to lash out with rage and, depending on his or her beliefs about how intentional these situations were, may launch a vendetta or attempts at revenge.

The Narcissist's Need to Idealize

Many psychotherapists who are unacquainted with working with narcissism will be uncomfortable with the devaluation or scorn (which must be handled neutrally and understood as the reaction to a felt blow to self-esteem) *and* with the idealization of the patient. The psychotherapist may be tempted to puncture the balloon the patient is

---

115   Rosenfeld, H., Ibid. describes this defensive maneuver in a way that leaves the reader with a clear sense of its deadly effect. Essentially, what happens is that the patient disowns the parts of the self that he or she does not admire (often aggression) and, instead, projects them onto the therapist, interpreting every consequent word and move by the therapist in this newly formed framework.
116   Such reactions are not uncommon and are especially noteworthy in psychoanalytical treatments. Such reactions will be discussed and additional citations noted in subsequent chapters. The negative transference reactions cited by Asch (Asch, S. S. (1976). Varieties of negative therapeutic reaction and problems of technique. *Journal of the American Psychoanalytic Association, 24*, 383–407) are especially worth reviewing.
117   Kohut, H. (1972). op. cit.; and Kernberg, O. (1975). op. cit., p. 229ff.
118   Kohut, H. (1972). op. cit.

inflating in the psychotherapist's favor, not realizing the close tie between the esteem the patient has for the psychotherapist and the esteem the patient has for himself. Unresolved self-esteem issues on the part of the psychotherapist may especially come into play here, so a psychotherapist may need to seek outside consultation, supervision, or even a stint of personal psychotherapy. The best response, without taking the idealized comments literally, is to appreciate and perhaps even thank the patient for the feedback.

"Healing" Pathological Narcissism

Not long ago, the prognosis for Narcissistic Personality Disorder was fairly negative. Even today, few patients with Narcissistic Personality Disorder come in on their own, usually coming for therapy because of troubles with others (such as marital, familial, or legal). Narcissists are also likely to resist taking medication and often do not benefit from medication when they *do* take it. With all the difficult transference and counter-transference problems associated with this population, many psychotherapists still consider this population untreatable.

Following application of our theory, however, psychotherapists can expect moderate to good results. This can often bring the patient out of being locked into narcissism and to a state where she is able to give and receive empathy and have relationships that are more satisfying. The crucial factor in a psychotherapist's success is recognizing that whatever the patient presents has something to do with self-esteem and, because they are still interlocked at this point, positive regard for others.[119] Of course, many special techniques that can be learned through instruction or experience or spontaneously created in special circumstances are involved; when a psychotherapist is in doubt about what to do, however, a safe, conservative strategy is to focus on careful listening and, regardless of what comes from the patient, to do whatever can be done to protect the senses of worth of both the patient and psychotherapist.

Because grandiosity was mentioned earlier as a particular sign of narcissism, it might be good to conclude with a treatment of this trait as an example. Grandiosity may be natural (*à la* Kohut) or defensive (*à la* Kernberg),[120] but whatever it is, it has at its root

---

119   Kohut, H. (1968). op. cit.; and Kernberg, O. (1975). op. cit., p. 227.
120   In Glassman, M. (1988). Intrapsychic conflict versus developmental deficit: A causal modeling approach to examining psychoanalytic theories of narcissism. *Psychoanalytic Psychology, 5*(1), 23–46. This article accomplishes two things. First, it provides a thorough discussion of the differences between Kohut's view of pathological narcissism (that a deficit is present in the self-structure) and Kernberg's view of narcissism (that the symptoms of narcissism are the results of an internal conflict concerning self-esteem). Glassman further shows how these theoretical views lead to differences in psychotherapeutic technique, with Kohut taking a much more supportive/remedial approach and Kernberg counseling that the resistances (such as grandiosity) must

an element of self-esteem. The psychotherapist might do well to take pains to see if this is the kind of defensive grandiosity that Kernberg describes, which covers over a feeling of emptiness and inferiority. Alternatively, psychotherapists must determine whether it is simply the basic building material of self-esteem (as Kohut might say) that needs to be hammered (quite gently) on the therapeutic anvil into a socially acceptable form of confidence and self-respect. Both approaches can fuel the patient in the future and keep him from being unnecessarily subject to counterattacks from others who feel that the grandiosity has eclipsed their own self-esteem.

---

be confronted (in the classical psychoanalytic style) if the therapist is to make any progress with the patient. Secondly, Glassman offers what he admits are some methodologically weak (though relevant) data supportive of the deficit explanation.

As you can see from reading our material, our approach is much closer to Kohut's. We think that confrontation, unless it is done accompanied with much support in the context of a very stable relationship and no sooner than by the middle of therapy, *almost always* produces the result of immediate termination of the therapy. It may be possible that Kernberg was influenced by a counter-transference reaction to patients with Narcissistic Personality Disorder that preceded the formation of his technique to confront negative treatments of the therapist's self-worth.

CHAPTER 10

RAPPROCHEMENT AND CHARACTEROLOGICAL DEPRESSION

S ome theorists associate rapprochement with borderline syndrome.[121] Because the borderline personality does not have firm boundaries, tends not to see people as encompassing both good and bad characteristics, has severe autonomy conflicts, and is so "stormy," we do not think the association of rapprochement with borderline pathology is appropriate. As stated in Chapter 4, the fit seems better for the characteristics of the earliest stages of individuation, or the hatching stage.

There is, however, a group of troubled people who do share important structural and emotional characteristics with the rapprochement child—the manic-depressive. The symptoms found in these people are not described in DSM-IV-TR under the Axis II dimension,[122] though they do represent a stable personality organization over time. Not being included in DSM-IV-TR's Axis II classifications is also indicative of receiving little attention by the health community; few people write about any disorders associated with this stage.[123]

The traits associated with the healthy development of rapprochement consist of losing the fear about connecting with another or losing the fear of engulfment. Another trait is

---

121   Especially following Kernberg, which has already been noted.
122   Unless one considers the inclusion of the Depressive Personality Disorder as noted in Appendix B of DSM-IV, which will be tested through later research and is not one of the commonly accepted personality disorders.
123   Considerable care, time, and discussion is devoted to the concept, however, in the chapter entitled "The Miserable Patient" in: Giovacchini, P. (1979). *Primitive mental states.* Northvale, N.J.: Jason Aronson, Inc. Otto Kernberg also talks of a similar stable depressive state, which he calls the "Depressive-Masochistic character structures" (and lists three types, including the "Depressive Personality") in his 1979 book (op. cit.), pp. 18–20.

sensing the self and others as wholes. Characteristic traits such as mood swings, some oscillation back and forth between independence and relatedness, and the beginnings of neutralized and even integrated affect, are all part of this development. The child at this stage is full of himself and, therefore, more willing to risk reconnection with caregivers. Similarly, the child has learned enough about frustration and hard knocks received when trying to go it alone that he is ready to enlist the help of others in the accomplishment of his goals.

Reconnection at this point, when boundaries have already been made very clear during the narcissistic phase, means reconnection to both frustrating (bad) and gratifying (good) objects. At the same time, the child has learned, in spite of his fears from the hatching phase, that he does not fragment or fall apart, even in the face of frustration. In a word, the child is ready to see self and others as wholes, rather than to split off parts in order to maintain a self in formation that has fluid boundaries.[124] The separateness of the narcissistic stage is maintained, so the whole self and the representation of the whole object are also seen as separate. Both self- and object-representation are therefore experienced as separate (but capable of being related) and whole.

Unfortunately, during the narcissistic phase, little development in complexities of affect occurs. Good empathic contact can increase such development, but throughout the narcissistic phase, the child is, on an emotional level, primarily concerned with gratification and feeling good (or even grandiose or perfect). The practicing itself is largely in the service of learning how to elicit gratification or to help the child learn that she can accomplish such gratification on her own. Relationships with others, which could give rise to nuances of feeling, are largely restricted to concerning what that person can do for the child, or, if frustrating, to how the frustrating object (person) can be removed from her path.

With rapprochement comes the beginning of integration of self-ambivalence and of object, *but in the context of separate wholeness*. Important implications follow. If the narcissistic child has become full enough of the self to possess a sufficient number of fairly independent mastery skills or has become tired of the frustrations of going it alone in the world and no longer needs to prove independence, fears of merger will be transcended. This is attendant on the successful completion of the hatching and narcissistic phases. The child is then able to reconnect with his or her caregiving objects.

The price paid for this evolution is that splitting is no longer possible; objects can no longer be seen as all bad or all good, nor can the self. Too much has been learned by the child since the early days of hatching; the child now knows that the same object who

---

124   See especially pages 272, 284, and the surrounding pages, in the previously cited work by Giovacchini for a more thorough discussion of the rudimentary type of wholeness we are talking about.

seemed to ignore him at times also, at other times, seemed to find him to be the apple of the eye. Reconnecting with a caregiver means rejoining a whole object, not parts of an object that are split along a perception of whether they are gratifying or frustrating. Because self-development seems to parallel the perception of objects, the child has also learned by now that she neither falls apart nor becomes *totally* and finally uncomfortable when she feels bad, nor does she experience a perfect bliss that lasts eternally when she is gratified. Just as the object can no longer be split, the self cannot be split, as the child now knows. In summary, the child learns, following her learning about separation during the period of normal narcissism, about the wholeness of objects and of self.

The wholeness of the child, however, remains emotionally primitive. One way to think of wholeness at this point is to imagine the good object glued to the bad object and the self that feels good glued to the self that feels bad. In other words, initial wholeness does not mean any quantum leap forward in emotional development (those leaps come later); instead, the caregiver is *experienced* at times as either a witch or an angel, and the self is experienced as either "on top of the world," or "been down so long it looks like up to me" (to borrow lyrics from an old country song).

Even a casual reader will instantly realize that the word portrait provided above sounds very similar to the description of the manic-depressive, whose character structure is so stable and resilient that many well-meaning psychiatrists tell such patients, "You will always be like this and must therefore plan on taking this medicine (usually lithium carbonate) for the rest of your life."

Psychotherapists who have worked with bipolar patients who are not psychotic, as those related to the rapprochement stage are not, tell us that the patient has a dim perspective and memory at any given time of the other (good or bad) emotional state. When he is in one of the moods, it is as if memories of the other state are of no use to him—they cannot be accessed for any kind of neutralizing perspective that would lend stability. Furthermore, it is reported that one mood state frequently follows the other, so that mood swings are part of the picture. Another typical symptom is that of a type of tension often acted out in nervous activity.

Giovacchini explains that, because little to no neutralization occurs just after the joining of the two self-states or object images, difficulties arise in the accompanying tension and anxiety that conflicts seem to create in the patient. Here the conflict is not between the superego and the id or between dictates of the conscience and the drives; it is simply between two organized ways of experiencing the self and others. Because the anxiety is still at a cognitively primitive level, the patient expresses it the way a child expresses anxiety, not with sophisticated words, but with physical tension and activity.

The same caregiver who seems at times to be so frustrating is now recognized as being the identical person as the gratifying mother. The same self that can feel so good is now recognized as having the identical identity as the self that can feel devastatingly bad.

Because emotional development does not seem to have followed the pace of intellectual and behavioral development, the two selves or the two object-representations almost seem to be glued together[125] rather than neutralized or made more complex with many shades of emotional grays. This allows a self that feels frustrated (bad self-representation) to approach a caregiving figure who might be perceived as feeling good for assistance. It also allows for some objective separation when the caregiving figure is perceived as feeling bad or frustrating.

Without a more integrated object representation (in which feelings other than frustration or gratification occur in some complexity of emotional states), and without a self that has progressed much beyond the narcissistic pleasure-seeking/rage-about-frustration attitudes, however, wholeness is a mixed blessing. It allows for more mobility in that the object can again be incorporated in the self's worldview without reemerging into selfobject, but it does not allow for understanding the self or the object much beyond the primitive bad (feeling bad, rageful, despondent) or good (feeling good, satisfied, energized).

Because self- and object representations are now whole, one ramification is that of deep mood swings between the two states. Splitting is no longer a possibility[126] now that the object has consciously been let back into the worldview, so the object is experienced with its wholly gratifying part leading the way, or vice versa, without neutralization.

Giovacchini points out that such emotional integration results in a strong state of tension as the two opposite emotional states are united. He also describes a grand conflict between the two self- or object states, with accompanying anxiety as a signal of the conflict. Unlike anxiety in maturationally advanced adults, this anxiety is not differentiated, nor is it neutralized. The conflict is understood only dimly, if at all. The resulting anxiety is therefore not the spoken cognitive anxiety of the neurotic or adult, but rather the physical anxiety or tension and agitation of the child.

Furthermore, one notices that the child, or an adult arrested in this stage, cannot remain exclusively in one emotional self-state for long because the person is now aware of his or her own wholeness. When feeling good is activated, then, feeling bad will soon follow.

---

125   Giovacchini suggests they are loosely held together with a great deal of tension (see previous footnote for relevant pages).
126   Except, of course, under regression.

Similarly, objects experienced as gratifying will soon, with the smallest provocation, be experienced as frustrating. The converse is true of the experience of the self or the object, as well. Once again, it is important to emphasize how the rapprochement child's wholeness remains initially binary, almost as if two opposite selves are somehow held together.

Other variations are also possible at this stage. For example, the child's experience to date may have been largely frustrating, so that the self that feels bad occupies more psychic space than the self that feels good. An imbalance occurs, with the feeling-good state being more easily swamped and, therefore, the more fragile of the two. Reciprocally, objects and self may have been experienced almost without frustration, so that the grandiose, feeling-good self (with object representations that almost always deliver satisfaction) dominates.

We might see here a model for bipolar illness or manic-depressive illness, and a psychodynamic explanation for manic states, in which the patient is so grandiose he almost cannot even imagine limitation or frustration. Stable depressed states that do not seem accessible to cognitive psychotherapy could also be explained by this stage. Of course, such stable psychological states are sure to have an effect on neural chemistry, and psychotropic medication may be part of the curative process for these disturbed mental states.

One of the chief tasks of the rapprochement stage is to get the child on the way to object constancy, which requires more than a sense of object permanency or wholeness: object (and self) constancy requires relief from the all-or-nothing experience of things, relief that comes with the neutralization and differentiation of affect. When things are operating as they should, the constant back-and-forth of the rapprochement child presents her with variations in feeling that are not all-good or all-bad. Furthermore, once again, the use of the object allows for the teaching (primarily through empathy, although also through idealized example) of differentiated, neutralized affect. For example, the child learns that she does not really hate a playmate and want to kill him, but that she is very angry because she believes the friend has acted unfairly and taken a favorite toy from her house without permission. If the child has a good-enough parent, the parent will probably help approach the playmate and his parents for the recovery of that beloved toy. The child finds, then, that her feelings change. Having the toy back in her possession, she no longer hates her friend and may even want to play with him, sharing the toy. The feeling has thus been neutralized both by discussion and direction given by the caregiver, and by the child's own experience of the effects of her behavior. Rather than hating her playmate, she may learn that she likes to play with him but must be a little careful to ensure that her friend does not walk off with any of her toys. The final feeling state described here is a mixture of feeling bad and feeling good, with components for each.

Many feelings, other than the basic ones, can be described similarly, as composed of different parts of gratification and frustration. Disappointment, joy, enthusiasm, envy, annoyance, and appreciation could be a few examples. If we are able, through distancing ourselves and reconnecting with others, to receive empathic understanding of the different ways we feel, we develop an ability to remain constant with ourselves and toward others. We may not always feel the same way at all times, but we are not tossed to and fro by extremes of feeling that might even lead to splitting-off other people temporarily or permanently. We are more able to remain in a steady relationship that encompasses some independence with a variety of feeling changes, depending on what transpires within ourselves and with others. This is a signal of being on the way to object constancy, as Mahler has described.

If, however, an experience has been largely frustrating, there is little pleasure to mix in with the pain. In fact, the experience may even create the feeling or need to hide any sense of satisfaction, as flimsy and infrequent as it is. In the mind of the person in the rapprochement stage, if the majority of experiences have been negative, it is also very likely that major caregivers may be deficient in some way, as well. Though stability may be achieved, it will be done by adapting to the misery of feeling regularly frustrated. Again, a defensive wall forms around the emotional state and prevents further development toward object constancy. The reverse is also true: If the vast majority of experiences has been satisfying, the person's view is likely to result in being unrealistically grandiose and optimistic. Because the rapprochement child is still so primitive and helpless, the only way he could have such a majority of positive experiences would be through the mediation of his caregivers. Experiencing little frustration provides little reason for the person to learn to care for oneself; instead, the person will expect for things to magically turn out as he wishes. Here, others might regard the personality as manic because it would usually be in a positive state, with little recognition of the less-rewarding side of life and with little disappointment to mix with the elation, showing no neutralization of opposites. Although the caregivers (and likely the internalized representations of them) would be nurturing, they would also likely be deficient in providing empathy so that the complexities of feelings could be learned, preferring instead to "fix" things themselves.

Difficulties at this stage of development *could* produce something that looks like either a Depressive Personality Disorder[127] or bipolar illness, with the *possibility* of either depression or mania predominating. Without neutralization and differentiation of

---

127   One study found strong support for such a personality disorder. See Gunderson, J. G., Phillips, K. A., Triebwasser, J., & Hirschfeld, R. M. A. (1994). The diagnostic interview for depressive personality. *American Journal of Psychiatry, 151,* 1300–1304.

affect, the structure of the personality would likely be stable, restricted, and intellectually concrete, with emotions leading the way.

Counter-transference Reactions and Therapeutic Techniques

People generally like rapprochement children because they are not very self-centered and show interest in other people. The same is true of reactions to manic-depressives, people with stable depressive personalities, and manics: people generally find them interesting, probably because of the return of object cathexis, which makes them feel valued.

Other counter-transference reactions (we are talking not of unresolved problems within the psychotherapist but of the standard reactions sucked out of the object by dyadic personalities) depend on the nature of the balance between the feeling states. Confusion is added to the interest of the psychotherapist when the patient seems to flip back and forth between extremes of emotion (and accompanying "driven" behavior) with little obvious outside to trigger the change. In fact, people who have manic depression are confused, too. A good psychotherapist would need to be unruffled by these changes, as would a good parent to the coming and going or emotional swings of the rapprochement child, at the same time seeking empathic explanations for the shift. These explanations might be communicated to the patient to help her better understand the shifts herself and might be used to manage the patient (as with all the dyadic character disorders described so far). Furthermore, as the good parent of a child of two to three years of age would know, the psychotherapist would realize something of the old proverb "one swallow doesn't make a summer." As sure as night follows day, a bad feeling state will be followed by a good feeling state, and feeling good one moment will not guarantee feeling good for any extended time after that. The psychotherapist who understands an arrest or deficit at this stage of development would maintain a larger perspective (which would also be protective of his state of calm) and would help the patient find a sense of equilibrium when she felt helplessly depressed or on top of the world with no apparent reason. With an understanding psychotherapist, grandiosity would be transformed, with help, into positive self-esteem, confidence, and an ability for the patient to act on her own behalf to increase satisfaction. Similarly, helpless frustration or despair would be understood and transformed into effective action to raise the patient's spirits, increasing self-esteem and confidence.

The grandiosity of the manic state is ineffectual and soon gives way to deep despair, in no small part due to the poor judgment of action exercised.[128] The good psychotherapist,

---

128   Again, the model being presented here predicts this sequence, as it sees people who are manic as having the type of concrete thinking typical of the 2½- to 3-year-old child.

like the good parent of an over-enthusiastic child, would help the patient channel the good feeling into actions that would maintain at least some of the good feeling and confidence. The "fall to despair" would now also be accompanied by the frustration and bad feeling of having to act for oneself rather than having things turn out well by "magic."[129]

The depressive patient is a little more compromised in that she is more fragile. Good experiences, such as the reception of good empathy or a good therapeutic session, can plunge the depressive character into despair: The fragile sense of well-being that activates the depressive side of the whole self dominates and sweeps away any good feeling. Unlike the healthier person who loses a loved one or job and grieves, experiencing depression for a while and then moving on, the miserable (depressive)[130] patient experiences the depression as central to his or her identity.

At the most basic level, the psychotherapist must, as a good-enough parent with children who have had a bad experience, refrain from simplistic cheering-up through cognitive approaches, which may work with healthier patients, by realizing that the miserable patient is likely to feel that the psychotherapist doesn't really understand his misery. Psychotherapists should not wallow in the bad feeling but might take a good long look at it, as a caregiver would with a hurting child of three years, communicating care and understanding and earning the right, eventually, to attempt problem solving. Even then, the psychotherapist may discover that the patient has a whole list of other complaints. The psychotherapist may become discouraged himself or begin to label the patient a help-rejecting complainer, a malingerer, or even a masochist. Truly depressive personalities are not that way by accident; they have had a lifetime of empathic failures, disappointments, and other hurts that need attention. Patience and an ability to withstand the depressive effect on the part of the psychotherapist are essential in the recovery of the miserable patient. Often very slowly, almost imperceptibly and gradually, the patient will begin to feel better and be able to tolerate more positive affects without automatic regression into despair. Even then, the psychotherapist must be ready to manage and maintain a perspective on erratic slides into deep depression that happen from time to time.

Often, the "miserable patient" will attempt to care for the caregiver. This is probably, in part, a replay of early childhood, when the child attempted, before she was able, to tend

129   The person with a bipolar personality, as well as the person with a depressive personality, *has* the ability to see the opposite self or object state, but simply cannot experience it. Thus, equilibrium remains minimally achievable to him, and the current self-state he is in (or object representation he is facing) seems most compelling. These characteristics are in stark contrast to the borderline personality, who, by using splitting, loses all awareness of the opposite state and has no perspective.
130   We are clearly sticking with Giovacchini's description, but including stable depressions of various stripes, such as a Depressive Personality Disorder, various types of bipolar disorders, and even stable unipolar depressions.

to a troubled parent. It may also be an attempt to gain insurance that the psychotherapist will indeed be able to help the patient. In either case, the psychotherapist must be able to tolerate these ministrations and recognize the positive element of attachment to the object intrinsic to them, without indulging the patient by accepting the caretaking as if he or she actually *needed* it. Rejection of the caregiving will most likely be experienced by the patient as an injury, though setting some limits by interpreting in terms of the past and reassuring the patient of the clinician's own well-being are good ways to redirect the patient toward her own needs, provided this is not done too abruptly by the psychotherapist.

Other Considerations

Still "on the horns" of two primary feeling states, the conscience or superego of the patient, like the young child, is likely to be ruthlessly black-and-white in its thinking. A good-enough psychotherapist will not attempt a "superegoectomy" but will try to listen and understand, still offering humane grounds between the two poles.

Psychotherapists who seek to include all personality disorders within one category (such as borderline), in our opinion, muddy the waters.*[131] Each patient needs a different response. It is our firm belief that the characteristics that are recognized within the borderline diagnosis of the DSM-IV-TR are very different from the characteristics we have been describing in this chapter. Until better discrimination between these two categories is made, it will be difficult to assess the widespread reports of frequent serious depression accompanying borderline diagnosis.[132]

As the patient with depression and a self-structure similar to that of the rapprochement child heals and moves forward in maturation, the psychotherapist will find that the patient will begin to notice the uniqueness of the psychotherapist and of other people for the first time. This recognition will be accompanied by an appreciation of the uniqueness of the self, as well. Attachments to third parties, budding attention to the parent who was previously in the background, and infatuations may all be signals that the patient has moved beyond rapprochement and dyadic relating and is now in the Oedipal (triadic) phase of development.

---

*   An imprecise understanding of the patient leads to an inaccurate diagnosis and a flawed treatment.

131   This is exactly what Kernberg does, as you can see by reviewing what he includes in this diagnosis, on pages 8–21 of his 1979 book (already cited many times).

132   Rogers, J. H., Widiger, T. A., & Krupp, A. (1995). Aspects of depression associated with borderline personality disorder. *American Journal of Psychiatry, 152*, 268–270.; Soloff, P. H., Lis, J. A., Kelly, T., Cornelius, J., & Ulrich, R. (1994). Risk factors for suicidal behavior in borderline personality disorder. *American Journal of Psychiatry, 151*, 1316–1323.

Summary and Conclusions

The rapprochement stage of pre-Oedipal development offers a useful model to understanding what stable depressions are like and how depression is unique. Several important accomplishments occur during rapprochement: the initial step of development in recognition of wholeness in self or object, the return of ability to recognize the object, the further consolidation of separateness, and the continuing growth of cognitive skills. This stage has associated weaknesses that also fit the psychopathologies described above. Concreteness has been mentioned repeatedly, as have the experience of anxiety as tension and a limited reference to an archaic superego that tortures the patient by constantly placing her on extreme opposite sides of a black-and-white dilemma. Although it was not labeled as such, ambivalence about themselves and others marks these patients. Each of these psychical deficits are maturational features of rapprochement and, with an arrest or deficit theory, help us understand the person whose depression just doesn't go away.

Cognitive therapies that "cheer up" and "look on the bright side" are outright dangerous with the patients under discussion in this chapter[133] because if they are successfully shifted to feeling good, a precipitous fall soon follows that can make the previous good feeling seem like an illusion and, therefore, place them in a doubly depressed state. A much safer strategy for the psychotherapist is to attempt to show empathy with the currently preeminent mood state to establish a connection with that corresponding part of the self. Eventually, the psychotherapist can serve as an alter ego when the patient is feeling so good that she defies common sense, or so bad that she is preparing to do herself harm.

One variation of the above recommendations is hinted at in the DSM-IV-TR category "bipolar disorder II," with qualifiers added to indicate either a depressed or hypomanic quality. Giovacchini spends almost all of his time on depressed qualities, explaining the personality structure of the depressed person by suggesting that his life experience has been primarily negative, so that feeling bad greatly dominates feeling good. The patient extends feeling bad even to the point that he hides feeling good, realizing that the positive state is quite fragile, vulnerable, and therefore subject to being swept away by the miserable-feeling state, leaving him bereft of hope. Though Giovacchini does not say so, his case example could be "reversed" to include those whose life experiences have been primarily good, leaving them with little sense of the misery, frustration, and bondedness that can also come with a balanced experience of life. These latter people, then, would fit the hypomanic description.

---

133 But such cognitive-behavioral approaches might be useful to a healthier population suffering symptomatic depression.

Treating self and others as whole persons rather than as objects to be ignored or treated as good or bad depending solely on how they gratify or frustrate is more appealing to most people, so stable depressed people are more likable. They also show connectedness, some empathy, and regard for others. These are all qualities that make this person more appealing as a patient (he or she better meets the psychotherapist's own narcissistic needs), even if the patient is miserably depressed. Some of these patients, whether due to lifelong habit or concern that the caregiver might fall apart and be unable to help, are actually successful in giving care to the caregiver.

Although all of the qualities or behaviors in the previous paragraph set the tone for a more positive counter-transference reaction on the part of the psychotherapist, it is important for the psychotherapist to have a clear idea of who he is dealing with. Because the pattern of depression is stable, no quick problem-oriented solution is likely to help. Most likely, the patient has a multitude of experiences that need to be addressed and neutralized. Unless addressed they will continue to make the patient ride up and down on the roller-coaster ride of extreme feelings.

The other patients with depression described on the pages of this chapter are dyadic persons who will invest almost all of their feeling and fate into one other person, much the way young children typically do with a parent. It is important for the psychotherapist to recognize and maintain boundaries and protect such patients from being lost, as that would prompt a devastating regression. The psychotherapist must also be prepared to deal with an archaic superego (the precursor of the more normal superego), which is invested with judgments that are extreme and accompanied by feelings that are equally intense. Learning to first tolerate the pronouncements of such a superego, and eventually to help a patient see more shades of gray and thus to become more humane, is all a part of the psychotherapy.

Indeed, developing greater emotional complexity and capacity through empathy and explanation is much of the work cut out for the psychotherapist with depressive patients. Just as the rapprochement child returns to parents for more information about how to cope with life and begins to deal with greater social complexity, persons stuck at this emotional stage must be given the same type of help. If they are not, perhaps the well-meaning psychiatrist portrayed earlier, with the pessimistic prognosis, will have been right after all.[134]

---

134   This remark is not intended to be a sarcastic dismissal of any genetic or biologic contributions to long-term depressions. Certainly, as Kagan and others have pointed out, there are constitutional factors that play a role in shaping the way a personality unfolds; see Kagan, J. (1988). The meanings of personality predicates. *American Psychologist, 43*, 614–620.; and Kagan, J. & Snidman, N. (1991). Temperamental factors in human development. *American Psychologist, 46*, 856–862. It is also hard to imagine a person functioning in an abnormal way for a long time without it affecting his body chemistry. Also, this is not meant to be a dismissal of the possible important use of antidepressant medications.

CHAPTER 11

ANTISOCIAL AND PARANOID PERSONALITY DISORDERS

Amongst the DSM-IV-TR list (as well as other clinicians' lists) of personality disorders are two categories that receive much concern but little psychodynamic attention and explanation: the paranoid and the antisocial personality disorders. The latter, the antisocial group, has been known previously by other names, such as psychopathic and sociopathic. Regardless of the names used for these categories, however, understanding of them has eluded clinicians for a long time. Indeed, this group of behavior disorders has long baffled psychiatrists, and the diagnosis "psychopathic personality" has come to be considered a wastebasket diagnosis.[135] One author has even gone so far as to argue that we need an entirely different system of psychology, as people with Antisocial Personality Disorders operate from a completely different set of rules than do most people.[136]

Important thinkers have struggled to place the antisocial personality within the developmental schema of accepted ego or psychoanalytic psychology. Kernberg, for example, clearly recognizes the role of a deficient or missing superego in the life of an antisocial personality,*,[137] With regard to the former, Alexander and Shapiro note that

---

*   Individuals considered to have an antisocial personality disorder have also been described as "psychopaths" or "sociopaths." It is true that this diagnostic entity, like all others, shows considerable variability related to the manifestations of the psychological deficits we shall articulate. Some become overt criminals, whereas others may function at a rather high level of personality integration. The latter might, for instance, make use of a combination of charm and a refined capacity for manipulation to be quite successful in business.

135   See pages 132–133 in Alexander, F. & Shapiro, L. B. (1952). Neurosis, behavior disorders and perversions. In F. Alexander & H. Ross (Eds.), *Dynamic psychiatry* (pp. 117–139). University of Chicago Press.

136   See Samenow, S.E. (1984). *Inside the criminal mind.* New York: Times Books.

137   Kernberg, O. Ibid. pp. 253–255.

Freud describes a criminal who acts from a guilty conscience "to express his crime and in this way he appeases his unconscious guilt and makes a bargain."[138] Because of this difficulty placing antisocial personalities, they are typically not placed in any particular developmental schema, particularly if viewed psychoanalytically. Kernberg describes them as one type of Borderline Personality Disorder[139] and, more specifically, as a sort of Narcissistic Personality Disorder.[140] Kohut's category of narcissistic behavior disorders[141] sounds very much like the antisocial personality.

Research shows that delinquents (many of whom have antisocial personalities) have a high preponderance of missing or dysfunctional fathers. Research also shows that children of parents who have antisocial personalities, raised apart since birth from their own parents, show a higher-than-expected rate of antisocial diagnoses,[142] which suggests a genetic or biological factor. A commission formed by the American Psychological Association in 1994 to study violence in youth, however, concluded that "[i]f persons have not initiated serious violent behaviour by age 20, it is unlikely that they will ever become serious violent offenders"; that "many youthful victims of violence are also involved in violent behaviour themselves, or at high risk of becoming violent during their adolescent years." Furthermore, factors implicated in etiology of violent behavior have their origins in "the early learning experiences in the family. They involve, [sic] (1) weak family bonding, ineffective monitoring and supervision; (2) exposure to and reinforcement for violence in the home; and (3) the acquisition of expectations, attitudes, beliefs, and emotional responses which support or tolerate the use of violence." Additionally, it was noted that "parental neglect may have an even stronger effect than physical abuse on later violence, as it appears to be more damaging to the subsequent course of youth development and involves three times as many youth."[143] These findings clearly illustrate that learning is an important factor as well (even recognizing that violence and antisocial personalities are not the same things).

---

138   Alexander & Shapiro, Ibid. p. 133.
139   Kernberg, O. (1975). op. cit., p. 115.
140   Kernberg, Ibid., p. 228.
141   Kohut, H. (1978). op. cit., p. 416.
142   Cadoret, R. J. (1978). Psychopathology in adopted-away offspring of biologic parents with antisocial behavior. *Archives of General Psychiatry, 35*, 176–184.
143   This study examines the roots of youth violence and highlights successful interventions. It is referenced in Elliot, D. S. (1994). *Youth violence: An overview.* Institute of Behavioral Science, University of Colorado—Boulder (pp. 1–3). Downloaded from www.cde.state.co.us/artemis/ucb6/ucb61092acl79942internet.pdf, 10 December 2008. For additional information, review the report "Youth and Violence: Medicine, Nursing, and Public Health: Connecting the Dots to Prevent Violence," published in December 2000 by the Commission for the Prevention of Youth Violence. A comprehensive clinical review, replete with psychoanalytical, biological, and social etiological as well as treatment considerations is to be found in J. Reid Meloy's classic text, *The Psychopathic Mind: Origins, Dynamics, and Treatment,* published in 2002.

Although genetics may play a role, we propose, from the psychodynamic perspective, that Kernberg and Kohut are correct in their statements, though perhaps not in the way they explain it in their work. Because it is widely accepted that the superego is the distillation of the object relationship between child and authority figure (most often with the father setting limits),[144] it makes sense that a child who has a missing, deficient, or defective (e.g., antisocial personality) father would either have little to internalize for a superego or that what would be internalized would offer poor guidance in the social world.

We know already, from the developmental theory presented in Chapter 4, that the father begins to play a more important part in the child's world around the time of hatching. He may increasingly offer an alternative safe harbor for the child to anchor in, away from the symbiotic orbit of the mother, during the practicing stage and beyond.[145] If the father is not there or is deficient in some important ways the child may attempt to move beyond practicing and toward rapprochement, but with important limitations. Certainly, the social interest of the rapprochement child would be present, as the child has now tired of the frustration of "going it alone," but the rapprochement would not lead beyond the dyadic realm (remaining simply caregiver and child), and there would be little with respect to object relationships to internalize for the superego's development needed for the next stages (particularly the Oedipal stage).

Is it any wonder, then, that the antisocial personality would share many of the features of the narcissistic personality, such as its superficial charm, grandiosity, lack of empathy for others, and devaluation of others? We might best think of the antisocial personality as caught midway between the practicing and rapprochement stages without enough fuel to make it to rapprochement.

A former prison psychologist with many years of experience stated that the psychotherapist must catch the criminal in his lies, while also showing empathy for the deficits he has experienced, to be respected by him.[146] This same attitude is counseled in other respects[147] and may, in fact, be similar to the curative idealizing transference that

---

144 Brenner, C., Ibid., pp. 111ff; St. Clair, M. Ibid. (Also see Chapter 6, "Edith Jacobson: An Integrated Model" (pp. 96–99) in St Clair, M. for a discussion on this.)

145 Blos, P. (1985). *Son and father.* New York: The Free Press (p. 116).

146 Weber, C. D. (1996). Personal communication. Weber served for years as the Coordinator of Outpatient Services for the Central and Southern Regions of the State of Michigan Department of Corrections. More than one study now indicates that group therapy, whereby an antisocial personality may be "caught" (confronted) by others who know his tricks as well as he, as well as supported by the same peer group, is the *most* effective form (superior to individual therapy) of treatment for this diagnostic category.

147 Huff, C. R. (1989). Youth gangs and public policy. *Crime and Delinquency, 35*(4), 531. Also see Samenow's book cited in footnote 136 above.

Kohut describes as transmuting.[148] Note that manipulative idealization, as in Scenario 7 of Chapter 1 with Richard and Dr. Arness, does not work.

If the above is true (and it does seem to match the nature of the antisocial personality and predict what will help), this type of personality disorder need not be left out in the cold or be regarded, as Kernberg regards it, as having a very poor prognosis.[149] As with the other character disorders, one needs to persistently and knowledgeably supply the missing ingredient to the deficient backgrounds (in this case, of both limitation and alliance) for the personality to mature. Without this understanding, antisocial personalities treated by psychodynamic techniques have a reputation for better learning to rationalize their behavior without making genuine change.[150]

Peck describes a "malignant" narcissistic personality in the same type of negative prognostic terms used by Kernberg.[151] He is, however, much more careful in describing, in later chapters, the danger of passing judgment on these people or in setting oneself up in a superior position. Kernberg is correct in pointing out the extreme difficulty in working with this diagnostic category, but psychotherapists have at times been swept away in the natural counter-transference reaction drawn out by the antisocial (narcissistic strain) personality and can therefore experience emptiness, scorn, and negativity toward the patient because such feelings have already been directed toward them by the patient.

Kernberg has described the paranoid personality as another form of the borderline personality.[152] Our contention is that this *cannot* be so, unless one construes all character (or personality) disorders to be Borderline Personality Disorders, as Kernberg sometimes appears to do. One instance of the Paranoid Personality Disorder is portrayed in Scenario 6 of Chapter 1. Although paranoid personalities can be amazingly intelligent, they are typically astoundingly simple from an emotional standpoint. This makes us think that paranoid personalities are at a more primitive level than most borderline personalities, and certainly (because we tend to agree with Kohut, and not Kernberg, that the narcissistic personality is the *high*-functioning borderline, if a borderline at all),[153] more primitive than the almost flagrantly secure and full-of-self narcissistic personality.

---

148   Kohut, H. (1984). op. cit. By "transmuting internalization," Kohut meant that the therapist at first supplied skills in the relationship that had not been taught or learned from early primary caretaking objects, so that eventually the patient is able to make these skills his own, filling the void and then being able to operate independently.
149   Kernberg, Ibid., p. 254.
150   Weber, C. D. (1996). Personal Communication.
151   Peck, M .S. (1983). *People of the lie: The hope for healing human evil.* New York: Simon and Schuster (p. 77ff).
152   Kernberg, Ibid., pp. 11 and 205–206.
153   There are many ways to consider this, but probably the simplest is to see where we have placed the narcissistic personality on the developmental continuum *vis-à-vis* the borderline personality, especially in comparison with Kernberg's placement. On another line of thinking, we have argued previously that the characteristics of the narcissistic personality are more highly developed than those of the borderline personality.

Unfortunately, as Scenario 6 points out, the simplicity of a paranoid worldview does not make treatment simple—quite the contrary. One way to think of the paranoid state is as of being midway between the symbiotic and hatching stages with that ubiquitous deanimated frozen wall around the core emotional structure, indicating a trauma, arrest, or deficit. What this means is that people with paranoid personalities trust no more than one person at a time, and this person is trusted completely (with blind trust), to help make experiential sense of the world and to cope. All others, as Melanie Klein's previously mentioned metaphor concerning this stage notes, are "not me"[154] and are, therefore, dangerous, malevolent objects. The confidant, however, is all-understanding and concerned with the complete gratification of the paranoid personality. We also notice, as the vignette with Jack Sanderson illustrates, that the paranoid does not know how to set proper boundaries and, once feeling understood, feels completely, symbiotically understood and tends to be ready to "spill all of the beans" to the psychotherapist. A beginning psychotherapist might pride himself on how well he has shown empathy to get an obviously difficult, suspicious, and untrusting patient to reveal so much, but here is the rub: the paranoid personality is so infantile that the patient simply did not know when to stop or set boundaries on his trust with a stranger and is soon likely to feel incredibly vulnerable and exposed. The more experienced psychotherapist will set limits on what the patient with paranoia shares, regulating the patient so that more is never shared than the patient can tolerate. If this does not happen, the paranoid personality, on later reflection, may wonder if crucial information has been given to a bad object.

As psychotherapists reflect on the characteristics of paranoid personalities, they will see that the all-or-nothing nature is a dead giveaway to the primitive origins of a patient's problems. Unlike the narcissistic personality, the paranoid personality fears, and can quickly become fused with, another person. The paranoid personality also *frequently* shows psychotic symptomatology, even if it is not central (such as ideas of reference, projection, and delusional thinking), whereas the narcissistic personality shows these symptoms only rarely, under regression.

With profound boundary problems, even empathy for the paranoid personality can become a double-edged sword. Patients may crave the fusion on one hand but, on the other hand, fear the opportunity for domination by the object, especially in the early stages of treatment. This is why a benign distance becomes the optimal stance, balancing the paranoid personality's need for understanding with his or her need for distance (which is interpreted as safe independence). Speaking of safety, if the pun is pardoned, it is a relatively safe subject to spend time discussing with the patient; patients with paranoid

---

154 *Á la* R. D. Laing.

personalities feel they are almost alone in a world of dangerous, strange, "not-me" objects, so calmness on the part of the psychotherapist and a verbal/behavioral recognition of the importance of safety (sometimes achieved through seclusion) is appreciated by the patient.

In summary, we see the Paranoid Personality Disorder as being one of the most primitive personality disorders (as is the schizoid personality), requiring intense energy invested wisely in the relationship on the part of the psychotherapist. The psychotherapist's intensity, however, is not for closeness, until the paranoid personality is *clearly* ready for it, but rather for protecting the safety and understanding (even later—though not too soon—being able to share that understanding with the patient) the cryptic existence of the patient. In a way, this is like establishing a symbiotic fusion in a very careful, gentle, and slow way, almost as if handling a burn victim, so that you, as psychotherapist, may eventually be part of the selfobject and help the patient to make sense of his or her world. If all this happens successfully, the patient, like others who make it successfully through symbiosis by getting what they need, will eventually begin showing the early signs of bracing, or "rolling away," that signal the beginning of the hatching stage of the separation/individuation stage of pre-Oedipal development.

Counter-transference Reactions and Psychotherapeutic Techniques

Therapists of the antisocial personality typically first notice the seductive nature of the patient's style of presenting himself. We find this akin to the wooing behavior of the rapprochement child. Like that child's, the antisocial personality's wooing has little substance to it. Unlike that child, the patient is typically not capable of complex, even triadic, relationships, but is best at seductive two-person relationships that often leave the psychotherapist feeling used, like Dr. Arness in Scenario 7 of Chapter 1. The psychotherapist must not be used or seduced but must show the boundaries of the rapprochement-stage good parent, which also encourages the patient to have ties with others that are not usurious and that draw the patient out of the dyadic thinking of "you and me against the world."

Treating the paranoid personality can leave a psychotherapist resonating with the patient's fear so that the psychotherapist often complains, "I feel like I am walking on eggshells." While important to address such typical counter-transference reactions, measured and planful care is essential if the psychotherapist is to help the patient feel safe and, at the same time, separate from domination. Allying with the patient enough to facilitate a symbiotic bond that allows the psychotherapist to help the patient maintain emotional equilibrium without the patient feeling weakened or dominated is a navigation over eggshells. When all else fails, unlike with other diagnostic groups, allowing separation is essential, as is promoting safety, whenever it can be developed.

CHAPTER 12

THE 'OEDIPAL CRISIS' AND ITS 'NEUROTIC' FALLOUT

A debate rages among Object-Relations Theorists and more traditional psychoanalytic thinkers about whether something different begins happening at the Oedipal stage of development or whether the problems that seem to originate with the Oedipal period can be understood by the development of the self during the pre-Oedipal stage.[155] Some psychoanalytical thinkers[156] seem to take a middle position, arguing that the drive-and-conflict theory of traditional psychoanalytic thinking is something that happens only when the self-system has not developed in a healthy way in previous stages.

Those who feel that problems begin to arise from only the Oedipal stage of development deny the very existence of biological drives (as if hunger or thirst did not affect behavior) and state that humans seek only object contact (generalizations are usually taken from a limited number of studies of infant behavior to bolster this claim). Those who take what we call a "middle position" state that drives result when the object-seeking is frustrated by faulty object-relations.

---

155 Because so *many* books have been written about Freud's concept of the Oedipal conflict and how neurosis can result (our favorite is still the Brenner book previously cited; still, abbreviated discussions have been found in college-level introductory texts, such as Lefton's, which is also already cited), we do not attempt to reiterate what others have already stated so well and in so many ways but rather to restrict ourselves to how Object-Relations and Self-Psychologists view the Oedipal stage, focusing particularly on innovative or variant ways these psychologists have of regarding the Oedipal stage.

156 Of course, Fairbairn is the perfect example of this, and many followed his ideas to one extent or another. See Fairbairn, W. R. D. (1954). *Object relations theory of the personality*. New York: Basic Books (especially pp. 137–161). See also: St. Clair, op. cit. (pp. 171–173 are especially clear in this regard.)

What seems clear is that, by the end of the rapprochement stage of development, the "feel" of (that is, the way that others perceive) the child or patient arrested at this point is different in some important ways. These differences in mood, behavior, or relatedness indicate personality organizations that are quite disparate and require different treatment approaches.*

First, the child who has achieved Mahler's type of object constancy has internalized "road maps" consisting of his or her experiential memories of how things worked in earlier significant relationships.[157] Such internalization enables the child to function with much less external control. It is as if the child now has a set of operational rules for approaching life that can be applied to different situations and/or relationships. The parent may still need to teach and to set limits, but constant management of the child does not mark the parent-child relationship. Conflicts, when they occur, are primarily internal on the part of the child rather than *in* the relationship, as they are with all previously described disorders.[158]

Second, the child's comprehension of the world is much more differentiated and complex than in previous stages. He or she is able to distinguish between different individuals rather than pulling at every individual to fulfill some need he or she has (selfobject needs).

Third, the child is secure and capable enough to attach to more than one other alter ego. Relationships are formed with, at first, one other person, and then later a series of people with whom the child enjoys a set of pleasures that is more restricted than that experienced with the first person.

Fourth, the child has more cognitive ability and emotional control. This enables the child to explore more interests, while modulating himself, outside the primary dyad.

Correspondingly, the psychotherapist dealing with a person whose troubles seem to date back to the Oedipal period does not feel herself caught up in the same intense two-person drama that she feels when dealing with a patient who has problems dating back to a pre-Oedipal stage. The Oedipally organized patient, having internalized so many "road maps," is more self-contained, so the transference is also more contained and feels much less intense. These patients complain of problems *within* themselves rather

---

*   In order to illustrate, even with respect to the clinical presentation and underlying psychopathology of adults, it is instructive to draw from observations of infants and children.

157   Chapters 1 and 2 of St. Clair's book (already cited) offer an excellent synopsis of convergence between the internalizations of object relationships and the building of structure, similar to that posited by Freud in all of his theories.

158   The article by Murray, op. cit., contains a review of the "two-person defense" idea. Although Murray is rather negative in tone throughout the article, please note that his negativity seems largely directed at those who would forget about all other types of defenses and be reductionistic, discussing *only* the defenses that show themselves in relationships.

than drawing the psychotherapist into a role designed to address a deficit. Furthermore, they *complain* or verbalize, rather than simply act in a fashion that magnetically attracts certain responses out of the psychotherapist. The psychotherapist feels a more neutralized atmosphere between himself and the patient, as well as one that can be discussed, differentiated further, and analyzed.

Fifth, the patient with the Oedipal conflict shows empathy. They are "decentered" from themselves and capable of recognizing needs that reside or originate in themselves or in others. The psychotherapist is not treated as having one valence, either gratifying or frustrating, but is seen as whole and complex. The back-and-forth movement of rapprochement leads to a give-and-take between psychotherapist and patient rather than to a blind taking from a selfobject.

Some of the "road maps" of this patient may be faulty or compromised, but the psychotherapist assists in making corrections. When faults occur at this stage, however, they seem to be between the self-seeking of the patient and whatever prohibitions the person has learned with various coping mechanisms (which could be called executive functions or defense mechanisms, depending on what one is dealing with), as Freud explained. It is not an imprecise descriptor to regard that person, when troubled, as one who has internal conflicts between what they want or wish for, on the one hand, and the limits of reality, be that social or physical, on the other hand.

Certainly, the earlier (pre-Oedipal) developments have been important building blocks to this new self-structure. The "nos" and the "yeses" the child has encountered as she has attempted to find gratification (be that lower-order physical gratification or higher-order interpersonal gratification) originally were parts of that child's or patient's object representations. Now, at the Oedipal stage, however, these are better organized and integrated, without the intense all-or-nothing types of affect of the previous stages. These object representations can usefully be thought of as superego directives, drives (or ambitions), and coping methods of the patient in question, rather than simply as one-to-one reproductions of something that happened in a dyad of caretaker and child.

The net effect for the psychotherapist is that she can be more separate, removed, and objective as she tries to help. She is also less likely to be instantaneously cast in an almost indelibly positive or negative light when she makes either a helpful or mistaken attempt to assist.

Other relationships can thus offer some neutralization of the intense need communicated in one fashion or another, unlike the patient trapped in a pre-Oedipal deficit. "Triangles" do form, where the patient may put the psychotherapist into competition with someone else (be that in the present or a memory of a relationship from the past), but the envy, jealousy, or rivalry is more limited and manageable for both patient and psychotherapist. Many more boundaries exist, as the child continued learning them from birth, again, unlike the patient fixated at the pre-Oedipal level of development.

Symptoms may exist in the Oedipal stage, as the fairly integrated internalizations now have a life of their own and may come into conflict, requiring some sort of compromise or defense; however, the child or patient now has internal (rather than needing strictly external) methods for dealing with these conflicts. Classically named defenses such as repression, reaction formation, emotional isolation, and so on, now seem to operate visibly (or, perhaps at first, invisibly).[159]

In a word, the psychotherapist feels relief and reward when he is dealing with these more highly developed individuals. Separateness and wholeness are not in question, although ways to seek gratification may be. Words as explanations from the psychotherapist have power rather than simply being experienced by the patient as impediments. Scenario 4 in Chapter 1 about Frank and Dr. Bell is a good illustration of the power of words with the more organized, neurotic individual.

In this stage, new issues have arisen with the child/patient's recognition of differences between others, as have new attachments to these different others. The child at the Oedipal stage is much more aware of same and opposite sex, wishing to either identify with one or to have all the gratification possible from the other. Simply having attachments divided between the two sexes reduces the intensity and makes talking about the attachments more feasible.

In summary, the problems of the neurotic personality, whose issues stem from the stage after rapprochement, have more-focalized and internal difficulties. The Oedipal patient also has more cognitive and emotional capability for addressing these problems. If there is an interpersonal problem, it is likely to be triadic, rather than dyadic, including some sort of competitive struggle among three people.

If healthy development proceeds, the patient's issues become even more specific to particular adjustments the patient must make to events that come up in life. A problem-solving and cognitive approach becomes more effective as the patient receives little to no contamination from the powerful and "boundary-less" difficulties originating in the pre-Oedipal periods of development.

---

159   Both the Alexander & Shapiro article (op. cit.) and the Brenner book (especially chapters 4, 5, and 6) offer explications of neurotic defenses, as does Lefton's (op. cit.) introduction (see pages 432–433), albeit in simplified form, illustrating again that Freud's ideas about neurotic defenses are almost "household words."

Eventually, if everything has gone well enough, the presenting problems take on an existential or life-stage issue character.[160] These issues may be difficult and may require a lot of "brain power," as well as empathy, on the part of the psychotherapist, but the psychotherapist is not wrapped up into the problem by the patient at this level of development. The patient's reserves and resiliency are also much greater, so that the pressure for quick solutions diminishes. No wonder psychotherapists prefer to work with patients like these. Focus can be warmly attached to the person and his specific problem or symptom; this is more palatable to both the clinician and patient than having to face a total restructuring of the personality, which is marked by significant confusion about where the problem begins and ends and is complicated by disorientation about whether the clinician is part of the problem or solution.

---

160   Similar to that classically described as in Erikson, E. H. (1959). Identity and the life cycle. *Psychological Issues*, 1(1), 1–171.

CHAPTER 13

PSYCHOPATHOLOGIES RELATED TO THE LATENCY PERIOD

T hough little is formally written about this relatively peaceful period following the storms associated with both pre-Oedipal and Oedipal development, we believe important developments take place during this time. Developmental psychologists such as Piaget, Flavell, and Gesell have discussed features of this period, talking primarily about cognitive developments.[161] Certainly, the image of the "little professor" who is curiously and methodically exploring her world, paying proper respect to her elders during the search, is a useful descriptive image to keep in mind, even if it is a stereotype.

Harry Stack Sullivan, an important figure in American Interpersonal theory on whose thinking some Self-Psychologists and Object-Relations practitioners drew, loved to talk of the importance of "chums" during the latency period.[162] One way to think of how peer bonds might be important is to consider them extensions of the development from dyadic to triadic (Oedipal) self-systems. This is especially helpful, particularly as the peer bonds assist the young person to further individuate from important others in his life, such as parents.

Some comments about the apparent quiescence of the latency period are worth making, for they shed light on this developmental stage. Following the successful internalization of "road maps" of important relationships that take conflicts out of the interpersonal relationship arena and make them intrapsychic (as occurs during the

---

161   Flavell, J. H. (1963). *The developmental psychology of Jean Piaget.* New York: Van Nostrand Reinhold.; Gesell, A., Ilg, F. L., & Ames, L. B. (1977). *The child from five to ten* (revised ed.). New York: Harper & Row.
162   Sullivan, H. S. (1953). *Conceptions of modern psychiatry* (2nd ed.). New York: W. W. Norton (pp. 49–56).

Oedipal crisis), many people are still left impaired with neurotic conflicts. These conflicts can draw strong sympathy from the bystander as he watches the misery of the neurotic who is at war with herself. The conflict is like those of the stereotypical conflicts that Freud described, where the person's primal sexuality would be unbounded if it could be (even possessing the parent of the opposite gender) but meets up with the stern, forbidding limits of an authoritarian parent whose impact is internalized and forms the rudiments of the superego. As an alternative, the aggressive drives of the patient might be disowned and repressed as contrary to the values of the superego. Yet these disowned impulses continue to slip through at inopportune moments, disguised as poor jokes or slips of the tongue that recurrently cost the patient goodwill from significant others or persons of influence in her society.

During latency, if the Oedipal period has been good enough, the child is not left with strong conflicts between parts of the self or between internalized selfobject relationships that keep him preoccupied with seeking solutions. Conflicts, if they exist, are minimal, and the latency-age child is able to turn his attention freely outside of himself. He becomes more complex than triadic. As Sullivan points out, the first relationships in the Oedipal stage (triadic) mimic the dyadic nature of the mother-child relationship in that the child has a special "chum" who is treasured, above all others, as an ideal collaborator who paradoxically helps the child reevaluate his relationship with his parents from a more objective distance.[163] In the latency period, however, we now have a fourth person in the picture who absorbs some of the energy that a dyadic person would have aimed completely at the primary caregiver and that a triadic person would have aimed at the internalized concepts of the primary caregiver (historically, the mother) and a secondary caregiver (historically, the father). The fourth person allows even further neutralization of emotional freight that could be experienced as quite stormy were it aimed at only one other person.[164] In addition, the fourth person allows for another possible internalized identification that will ultimately allow the child even more choices about how to be than if he identified only with parents.[165]

---

163   Sullivan, Ibid., pp. 43–56.

164   Blos argues that the latency period offers the emerging young adult a second chance to rework conflicts from earlier in life, incorporating further differentiation and neutralization. See: Blos, P. (1967). The second individuation process of adolescence. *Psychoanalytic Study of the Child, 22*, 162–186.

165   The relationship with society is further cemented as well, as Sullivan points out (see Sullivan, Ibid., p. 49.). In a different context, the psychoanalyst Jonathan Slavin claims that it is just this movement away from parental figures that makes psychotherapy quite difficult in a similarly (though older) group of adolescents: Slavin, J. H. (1996). Readiness for psychoanalytic treatment in late adolescence: Developmental and adaptive considerations. *Psychoanalytic Psychology, 13*(1), 35–52.

Furthermore, as the long latency period continues, a series of special "chums" may become elaborated across extended periods of time (until they move away or lose their usefulness) or the development of a peer group that has fifth, sixth, and even more significant persons in it. Each of these new relationships gives the child more experience with mastering the social world and further expands the choices for identification with skills and ways of being.[166]

If the latency period continues without major trauma until the onset of adolescence, when sex, the search for identity by sorting through a catalogue of fervent identifications, and some of the problems remaining from the dyadic period are resurrected through pair-bonding (particularly with the opposite sex) become important, the child becomes comfortable with self and with persons of the same gender, at least. The child's internal conflicts are also likely to be much more circumscribed and less intense at this point.

The successful latency-age child is more outgoing, less intense, and more complex than the successful Oedipal child, who tends to have more single-minded foci, be less outgoing, and often be quite intense. Many of the conflicts felt by the latency-age child are largely internal and felt *in* the relationship only minimally. The latency child will draw more fleeting and ephemeral reactions in relationships, as their remaining conflicts are not only more internal but also more neutralized and better controlled.

When something goes wrong in the latency period, the child (or arrested adult) can become socially phobic, possibly demonstrate lively neurotic conflicts, and become somewhat preoccupied with himself.* Other people may experience the person arrested in the latency stage as overly dependent or enmeshed with his family of origin and its expectations.

When things go right in the latency period, few basic developments are left to go awry. The troubled adolescent (whose previous development was basically sound) may have some trouble with gender identification, identity, and intimacy. She is unlikely to experience dysthymia (formerly and still sometimes called neurotic depression), however, although she may experience low periods and the grief that comes with a loss.

The latency period is instructive in that it further illustrates how the problems a person experiences become more circumscribed and more internal. The problems are not as disruptive in interpersonal relationships and are less fundamentally disturbed. With the benefit of having established and profited from a series of close relationships, the child

---

* This optimal trajectory and associated outcomes lead to a more cohesive character/personality structure—unlike what is seen in children, adolescents, or adults with dyadic character disorders.

166 See a discussion of various developmental tasks for this stage as noted in Freedman, S. (1996). Role of self-object experiences in affective development during latency. *Psychoanalytic Psychology, 13*(1), 101–127.

or adult who has successfully transversed the latency period is also more likely to be able to show a larger range of empathy. In short, patients with troubles relating to the latency period or later stages are even more likeable than those from preceding periods and are easier to work with. Their cognitive development has not been intruded on by powerful emotional conflicts, and they have had more time to mature intellectually without drastic interference, so their problem-solving abilities are greater than those of patients whose problems began at earlier stages of life.[167] Consequently, psychotherapy tends to be brief, and cognitive psychotherapy works more effectively. Group psychotherapy is experienced as less of an injury at this stage than at earlier stages and can often be used quite effectively.

Diagnostically, persons with difficulties stemming from the latency period do not warrant an Axis II diagnosis and often seem to fit the categories under adjustment disorders. Other diagnoses that sometimes occur for this stage are the social phobias, identity disorders, and the diagnoses resulting from special conditions such as post traumatic stress disorder or psychological conditions caused by medical disorders. In this stage, bonding with a psychotherapist, particularly one of the same sex, typically happens quickly, and problems are solved with rational skills more often than not.

The relative quiescence of the latency period is, therefore, rather misleading and deserves much more attention than it generally has received: We should not be lulled into assuming that all is well. Still, as has been noted, considerable consolidation of the (optimal) gains from previous stages occurs at this juncture, as does additional development. The relative quiescence is, therefore, simultaneously both apparent *and* real. It serves as a useful "way station" from the vicissitudes of earlier developmental periods on the road to greater identity consolidation. The relative degree of respite from psychical turmoil belies the potential storminess that, at the least, can potentially be so emblematic of adolescence proper. It is to this developmental epoch and its vicissitudes that we now turn our attention.

---

167   See page 434 in Lefton, Ibid., for a graphic summary of why this is true.

CHAPTER 14

ADOLESCENCE AND ITS LEGACY

Any hairline fractures that exist in the girders that are the framework of the personality structure, or even in small cracks in the foundation that binds the organization of the self together, appear as gaping holes and dangerous hazards during the developmental period that today we term "adolescence."[168] A glance at Erikson's classic description of a psychosocial theory of development shows that Stages 5 and 6 probably fit this age group best, at least as it is defined today.[169] Erikson saw the crisis facing the person in his fifth stage as the attempt to form a coherent identity instead of being undifferentiated and chameleon-like. Erikson's sixth stage involved the capacity to form meaningful intimate relationships instead of becoming isolated.

Because the concept of adolescence is a creation of the 20th century and was not important in literature before then, it is a relatively new concept and one that is still in flux.[170] Originally, the term referred to a period of time between the end of childhood and the onset of true adult responsibilities. Quite often, it seemed to refer to persons of junior high and high school age. Sometimes, however, it was unclear whether the term might refer to the college-aged person, who might act like an adolescent and still be totally dependent on his parents or other adults. Historically and anthropologically, adulthood began sometime around the time of puberty, with accompanying rites, to mark the shift into being regarded as a full adult.

---

168   Blos, Ibid. as already mentioned in a footnote in the preceding chapter, views adolescence as a time to rework conflicts from earlier developmental periods. Furthermore, he, somewhat like Fairbairn, sees drives during this period as a *result of* the adolescent's need to gain distance from previous conflicts and attachments.

169   Erikson, Ibid., pp. 88–97.

170   A somewhat different point of view is outlined elsewhere, with the concept of adolescence being traced back to ancient Greece, but with acknowledgment that the concept has taken on entirely new energy and meaning in the 20th century. See: Slap, G. B. & Jablow, M. M. (1994). *Teenage healthcare*. New York: Pocket Books (pp. 1–13).

Even today, the boundaries of adolescence are not clear, as the college students of today are not veterans returning from war, nor necessarily preparing for a career. Nonetheless, during adolescence, two important developments that echo earlier development take place: individuality and the capacity for closeness. It is important to remember that autonomy and individuality are not the same thing, as the latter requires a consolidated identity, yet both strive toward independence. The intimacy and the relatedness of the dyadic child are also not the same thing, as the former *requires* individuality, but the latter does not, yet each has the characteristic of human closeness.

When people see adolescents oscillating back and forth between their needs for support and their attempts at independence, they might mistake such vacillations as symptoms of the fledgling attempts at independence first seen in the hatching stage. It is our contention that this mistaken impression is one reason that so many adolescents are wrongly given the diagnosis of Borderline Personality Disorder or are said to have strong traits of that type of personality organization.[171]

It is true that if a person reaches adolescence with the conflicts of hatching and rapprochement not fully resolved, those conflicts will be reawakened, but with the extra cognitive skill of someone in their teens and the extra energy released by the hormones of that age.[172] If the adolescent truly has a borderline feature, however, he will have lasting symptoms of the borderline, not just a conflict about independence and identity.

Learning to make the discrimination between normal adolescence and Borderline Personality Disorder is critical to the psychotherapist's understanding of healthy adolescence and what type of mental or emotional conflicts can arise from adolescence alone, with all previous development having been adequate. One crucial distinguishing feature is that healthy adolescents are not dyadic, other than for brief periods of time and in serial fashion. The healthy adolescent gains extra material to "edit" for his own identity by forming a series of intense bonds (often quite idealized).[173] Each of these attachments also draws the adolescent further away from his parents and more toward his peer group or even himself. Parents often have a hard time adjusting to this (sometimes not for the best of reasons, such as diversion of marital energy from a bad marital relationship into the relationship with the child); furthermore, if the parents are especially authoritarian or possessive, the teen is likely to move toward alternative attachments with all the more

---

171   Although it is only a beginning, we believe that DSM-III and following versions were both correct and struck blows against incorrect labeling of children and adolescents when they required an age of 18 to be achieved before an Axis II personality diagnosis could be given.
172   See Lefton, Ibid., pp. 316–318.
173   Slap and Jablow, Ibid., p. 12.

vengeance and seek autonomy even more rebelliously, appearing, superficially, to be irrational.[174]

A healthy adolescent, however, does have some sense of who she is and is able to verbalize her remaining doubts about her identity. She is also able to form attachments with boundaries—attachments that are not driven and contaminated by powerful lower-order needs (such as for security, self-esteem, etc.). If one takes the time to discuss with her what appears to be almost flighty preferences and overnight changes in bonding, appearance begins to give way to meaningful form in the sensible landscape of experimentation (unlike the "anything goes" exploration of the young child).

Consequently, psychopathology that is caused strictly by trauma or deficiency in adolescence has that same very circumscribed, limited nature to it. Adolescents may be disappointed in some crucial relationships and tend to increasingly withdraw rather than form lasting intimate interpersonal relationships, yet the psychological difficulty is usually not a deep-seated one. Often, an unhealthy tendency begun in adolescence can be overturned relatively easily at a later date, if others seek out the patient or if the patient receives enough support. Similarly, an ambivalent or poorly consolidated identity can often be pulled together with the integrative listening ear of a wiser older adult (these days, often a psychotherapist) or through identification with someone else who, in her own life, seems to successfully pull together all the diffuse strivings.[175]

If, however, the problem is one with true roots in an earlier stage of development and is only making an appearance in adolescence, the resolution of the problem will be the more-encompassing problem typical of that earlier developmental stage. The symptoms will be wider in scope and more likely to show themselves in intense ways in relationships with others.[176]

These are especially noteworthy considerations given contemporary trends to pathologize elements of childhood and adolescent life that do not accord with adult-

---

174   The relationship between parental control and adolescent adjustment is not simply a linear one. Moderate control seems to work best, while excessive or missing parental control are deleterious: Kurdek, L. A. & Fine, M. A. (1994). Family acceptance and family control as predictors of adjustment in young adolescents: Linear, curvilinear or interactive effects? *Child Development, 65,* 1137–1146.

175   The therapy is likely to be short-term and easily disrupted, however, as Slavin (Ibid.) points out, because it threatens the burgeoning adult identity of the adolescent. A similar point is made in: Erlich, H. S. (1988). The terminality of adolescence and psychoanalysis. In A. J. Solnit, P. B. Neubauer, S. Abrams, & A. S. Dowling. (Eds.), *The psychoanalytic study of the child, 43,* 199–212.

176   Slap and Jablow (Ibid., p. 7.) report that "recent research suggests that up to 40 percent of American youth progress through adolescence smoothly, without much storm and stress. The other 60 percent experience varying degrees of confusion, frustration and uneasy change." Even if not all of the 60 percent are dealing with leftover conflicts from earlier stages of development, these statistics give us some idea of how many people make it to the adolescent stage of development with relatively sound personality structure.

centered definitions of proper, "appropriate" behavior, conduct, or comportment. It is increasingly, and most regrettably, the case that adolescents are subject to ever-advancing pressures to be accountable to adult norms—at least in the United States (rather like earlier historical moments) rather than appreciated for the remarkable psychological, social, and biological (trans)formative processes that structure this unique developmental period. Greater sensitivity to the requirements and pressures acting *on* adolescents on the part of adults (parents, teachers, mental health practitioners, etc.) would go a long distance in redressing contemporary leaps to medicate, hospitalize, or otherwise respond coercively and stridently to the *Sturm und Drang* of adolescence and the wide range of expression of adolescent angst that can be vented.

Such punitive responses may serve only to further exacerbate the already precarious sense of identity cohesion, esteem, and competent efficacy of the normative adolescent. This, in turn, has the potential to aggravate the already tenuous hold on abiding object ties from preceding stages already strained under the aegis of the adolescent edition of "rapprochement." What may be called for is, as signified in the title of a book by the psychoanalyst Joyce McDougall, a "Plea for a Measure of Abnormality."[177]

177   McDougall, J. (1980). *Plea for a Measure of Abnormality.* New York: International Universities Press.

CHAPTER 15

ADJUSTMENT DISORDERS, LIFE CRISES, AND MATURATIONAL ISSUES

An adage has it that "Into every life, some rain must fall." Many such sayings exist to suggest a perspective on life that accepts the ups and downs. It is one thing to feel a little blue, another to feel chronically blue or depressed, and still another to feel so desperately helpless and hopeless that taking one's life seems like it might be a relief.

If a person makes it through the developmental stages until adulthood with a basically sound personality formation, the only type of emotional and cognitive stress he is likely to experience (except perhaps in situations of extreme stress, when anyone might temporarily regress even to a psychotic state) would be that caused by particular life events. Two common examples might be the depression-like grief that follows the loss of a loved one and the expansive, energetic feeling that could come with a major job promotion or winning a lottery.

Medical problems also can provoke significant regression, requiring major adjustments, depending on the problem and the treatments involved. For example, head and spinal injuries can initiate personality changes, some of them permanent. Occasionally, medications used to treat patients have psychotropic side effects—the drug Interferon, for example, which is used to treat several otherwise untreatable conditions—with "depression" and "flu-like symptoms" as possible side effects. Furthermore, medications and treatments can interact to produce mental health effects, particularly when several physicians are involved in the prescribing and no one is overseeing all medications administered. In general, the "passivity" associated with medical conditions, along with potential bodily changes, including cosmetic ones, may prompt anxiety associated with a (feared) regression to an earlier, dependent state as well as a narcissistic injury to one's sense of self-esteem, bodily integrity, physical beauty, and so forth.

The key to identifying an adjustment problem is recognizing that the patient gets better relatively quickly with basically commonsensical solutions to problems. The patient may require support or guidance for a time but respond without any obvious intrusions of other mental conflicts. Harry and Dr. Leving in Scenario 5 of Chapter 1 illustrate the quick recovery of an adjustment disorder.

When a patient does not get over what originally seems like an adjustment problem in a reasonable amount of time and with the expenditure of a reasonable amount of resources, the psychotherapist should begin to suspect that the adjustment problem is really an overlay onto a larger psychological problem. In this case, in a sense, the adjustment problem calls attention to the underlying problem—not "getting over" grief in two years, for example.

We have been told that the Chinese character for crisis means both danger and opportunity. We certainly see such a double meaning at work in Erikson's brave attempt to map out fairly inevitable crises in human development. Crises do exist beyond the central, commonly experienced problems encountered in normal maturation. For example, a young person may have an opportunity to travel that will take him away from the security of what he knows and will not likely return to soon. Married adults may face the crisis of divorce and react in ways that are creative for themselves and their children or may become emotionally crippled and crippling for life. An opportunity for a new job or career that might entail financial or other risks may come, offering, despite the risk, the possibility of bringing someone out of an emotional rut he thought he'd never escape.

As the classical Chinese book referenced in *Change*[178] suggests, each crisis starts with confusion. Many people are so dismayed by the confusion that they quickly retreat to the safety of the known. Those who can tolerate the ambiguity and allow themselves to become confused or torn by ambivalence, however, are likely to grow stronger and wiser as a result of facing the crisis.

Two things are noteworthy in the healthy person dealing with a normal life crisis. One is a greater likelihood to risk personal change if it also means personal growth. The other is facing the crisis without becoming bound up in unresolved issues or psychological

---

178   Watzlawick, P., Weakland, J. H., & Fisch, R. (1974). *Change: Principles of problem formulation and problem resolution.* New York: W. W. Norton.; and Mahoney, M. J. (1994). *Human change processes: The scientific foundations of psychotherapy.* New York: Basic Books.

processes indicative of failures for the purpose of reaching certain milestones in the formation of the human personality.

Life crises, like adjustment problems, can be magnets for drawing unresolved problems to the surface. If a person has never really thought for herself but has never had a problem because her life was laid out in a fairly predictable or even rigid fashion, she may never have had the opportunity to develop what Winnicott calls the true self[179] but has, rather, learned to please the authority figures around her. If someone like this were faced with a dilemma that did not have the dictates of authority surrounding it, she might become caught up in rumination and other obsessive-compulsive defenses as she seeks the "right" (translation: authorized) answer. Here, the problem would go much deeper, to what Winnicott called the false self and its cure. The life crisis could present opportunity, even in this case (with the right help), but that opportunity would likely be one that would develop over the long term, rather than simply growing out of the crisis at hand.

Life crises often are best faced when someone has another person to listen empathically, even if that other person does little more than reflect what the person in crisis seems to be saying. It is sometimes hard to hear oneself, especially at a deep level, and a good listener can often reflect accurately what he hears coming from the heart of the person in crisis.[180] Other times, someone who has been in the same or a similar situation can offer words of wisdom that are helpful to a person in crisis. These words are especially likely to be listened to if a good empathic bond has been formed between the two people and if the person in crisis finds the other person admirable. Again, if the life crisis has shaken loose an unresolved conflict from an earlier developmental stage, the conflict from an earlier stage can have a way of intruding and making the "simple" following of advice rather difficult.

All of us struggle with the meaning of life, and Erikson's last two stages (as do the millions of persons across the globe who seek meaning in various religions and philosophies) particularly demonstrate how important finding meaning can be. Frankl oriented many mental health practitioners with his belief (which he obtained from his experience in a concentration camp) that people "starve" for meaning and will do almost

---

179   Winnicott, D. W. (1965). Ego distortions in terms of true and false self. In *The maturational processes and the facilitating environment*. New York: International Universities Press (See especially pp. 140–152). (Original paper published in 1960.)

180   Carl Rogers founded an entire school of psychology on this principle, primarily with his work among a university population (people who have reached this level of teaching or study were among the least developmentally disturbed of the population). Many works summarize his approach, but none better than one of his earliest and most seminal articles: Rogers, C. (1946). Significant aspects of client-centered therapy. *American Psychologist, 1*, 415–422.

anything to find meaning that will make their understanding of their lives cohesive.[181] Again, sometimes it is hard for us to hear what heart, gut, mind, and soul are saying about a matter, but a good listener can be enormously helpful, allowing us to clearly hear ourselves, especially if that listener does not have deaf spots originating from an agenda of leading us in a certain direction. A guide who can listen and tell of her own experiences with similar value conflicts also can be enormously helpful.

Whether life crises and maturational issues constitute either the cultivation or protection of mental health is a matter of debate. Adjustment problems are included in the DSM-IV-TR, as they were in earlier versions, so they are considered by professionals to be mild forms of mental disorder. As such, modifications to the treatment approach are warranted. Psychotherapists often help people with these mild disorders, offering assistance more effectively if they are sensitive listeners, truly concerned with helping a person develop their own unique identities rather than seeking recruits to a personal point of view, if they have coped successfully with some adversity themselves.[182]

---

181 See Frankl, V. E. (1960). Paradoxical intention: A logotherapeutic technique. *American Journal of Psychotherapy*, *14*, 520–535. See also, Frankl, V. E. (1959). *Man's search for meaning*. Boston: Beacon Press.

182 Some classical studies that address these issues include Bergin, A. E. (1966). Some implications of psychotherapy research for therapeutic practice. In G. E. Stollak, B. G. Guerney, Jr., & M. Rothberg (Eds.), *Psychotherapy research: Selected readings* (pp.118–129); and Truax, C. B. (1963). Effective ingredients in psychotherapy: An approach to unraveling the patient-therapist interaction. *Journal of Counseling Psychology*, *10*, 256–263.

CHAPTER 16

'ROYAL ROADS' TO A CURE: USE OF TRANSFERENCE AND COUNTER-TRANSFERENCE

No psychoanalysis can proceed any further
than the neurotic complexes of the psychoanalyst permit.

—*Sigmund Freud*

It is rare when a supervisor can help a psychotherapist "unblock" a stalemate in her psychotherapy with a patient by simply providing information to be shared with the patient. When these infrequent occasions occur, it is probably accurate to consider that what is happening is education, as opposed to psychotherapy.

More typically, therapeutic impasses occur when the transference, counter-transference, or both are poorly or incompletely understood by the clinician. Like an analogue for the decentering process that Basch describes as having applied to himself as the analyst,[183] a good supervisor or consultant can help a psychotherapist gain a perspective on the interpersonal events taking place between practitioner and patient that have led to a stoppage in the flow of the therapeutic process.

It bears repeating that, as Basch describes simply in the same book,[184] transference refers to the process whereby a patient "transfers" attitudes toward self and others from

---

183 Basch, Ibid., pp. 148–149.
184 Basch, Ibid., pp. 137–138.

one situation to another. Classically, most transferences have been discussed as originating in one of the parent-child relationships.[185]

Practitioners of Object-Relations Theory and of Self-Psychology use the concept of transference in essentially the same way that it is used in traditional psychoanalysis, except that they view transference possibilities as more complex and extensive.[186] In the Object-Relations or Self-Psychology Theory, one particular patient may be seen as being capable, even likely (especially if she is personality disordered) of directing several transferences toward a psychotherapist in a narrow expanse of time. This is distinct from the more traditional perspective, which would view the transference as more uniform and unchanging than does traditional psychoanalysis, as in a "father-daughter transference," for instance, across the intensity of the analysis. This would then be emblematic of the entire complex of the patient and constitute the major focus of the treatment. In discussing Kernberg's analysis of the treatment of Narcissistic Personality Disorders, Summers describes how a psychotherapist may be on the receiving end of opposite types of transference in alternating moments.[187] As he concludes his chapter on Kernberg, Summers gives several illustrations of patients who may employ diverse transferences, one after the other, in the same session with the same psychotherapist. By contrast, case discussions in more traditional Freudian psychoanalysis would usually present the case as if the patient transferred one set of perceptions or attitudes (such as the ubiquitous stern, forbidding, authoritarian father) into the current therapeutic relationship(s).

Historically, counter-transference was viewed as the blockage or misdirection of psychotherapy coming from unanalyzed reactions on the part of the psychotherapist. If a whining and complaining patient evoked an angry and uncompromising attitude that influenced the psychotherapist's approach or interpretations, one would begin to talk about the counter-transference reactions of the psychotherapist. Such a situation might occur as the psychotherapist deals with her unmodified needy girlhood reactions to the supplications of an overly dependent, perhaps even hypochondriacal, parent. Counter-transference was regarded at worst as an enemy or at best as a distraction, to be dealt with in the psychotherapy the psychotherapist received. Counter-transference was regarded as a filter or set of blinders that prevented the clinician from seeing the patient as he was

---

185   See Lefton, Ibid., p. 542; Winnicott, D. W. (1949). Hate in the countertransference. *International Journal of Psycho-Analysis, 30*(2), 69–74; Murray, Ibid., p. 36.
186   See the superb historical review on pages 9–39 and the excellent review of the many nuances and uses of counter-transference in the "total" sense in Tansey, M. J., & Burke, W. F. (1989). *Understanding countertransference: From projective identification to empathy.* Hillsdale, N.J.: The Analytic Press.
187   Summers, Ibid., p. 209.

really presenting himself because issues from the psychotherapist's own past cloud the issues she "hears" being discussed by the patient.[188]

Beginning with Winnicott's landmark essay,[189] counter-transference was seen in a wider context. Although the old definition was *included* in the new understanding, Object-Relations Theory, and later Self-Psychology, began to reexamine counter-transference reactions (mainly affective, although they might include sensory, cognitive, or other data) that would be drawn out of almost any psychotherapist by a particular patient. Winnicott presented a case in which, much to his surprise, he began to feel hatred toward a patient.[190] He discussed his aggressive feelings not in terms of some unresolved conflict of his own that thwarted his therapeutic neutrality but as the patient's unconscious ability to stir feelings in him that were probably similar to those expressed by the patient's mother.

In his book *The Collected Papers on Schizophrenia*, Harold Searles[191] amplified Winnicott's vision of counter-transference to include almost any nuance of feeling the psychotherapist might experience. Rather than urging the repression of these feelings in the service of a neutral or benign presentation by the psychotherapist, Searles's idea was to use the psychotherapist's reactions to provide further information about the patient. Thus, if a normally caring clinician suddenly began to feel disgust with his patient, the clinician now might wonder if he were experiencing the patient's own disgust with himself, experiencing a developmentally low form of behavior that the psychotherapist had learned to repress as part of growing up, and even wonder if the patient were rekindling an emotional reaction in the psychotherapist that dated back to an old relationship in the psychotherapist's life.

The wider understanding of counter-transference has been especially useful in the treatment of patients whose problems date from a time in their lives when their relationships were dyadic, as opposed to triadic or even more complex. Unresolved problems from these pre-Oedipal stages often resulted in personality disorders (such as the narcissistic, schizoid, or borderline personalities). Using Kohut's language, the person at a pre-Oedipal stage in her development could be thought of as a selfobject. This would mean that the child had not yet developed the "boundaries of the skin" to determine identities and be conceived as some other person (from the adult perspective) as part of their own

---

188 Again, see Tansey & Burke's (Ibid.) excellent historical review referenced in footnote 181 (this chapter).
189 Winnicott, Ibid., (1949). Note that Tansey and Burke (Ibid.) find the roots for a more "total" interpretation and use of counter-transference going back to the early work of Helene Deutsch and see others, such as psychoanalyst Theodor Reik, as contributing early alternative explanations to the "counter-transference as a block" idea.
190 See previous footnote.
191 Searles, H. (1965). *Collected papers on schizophrenia and related subjects.* New York: International Universities Press.

regulatory and gratifying self-system. During the pre-Oedipal stages of development, most of what transpires is done nonverbally, as if the caretaking adult is a mind-reading alter ego. The caregiver of the child in one of these stages, or the psychotherapist of the person arrested in one of these stages, would then sense rather than hear the needs and state of the child or patient. Through behaviors or expressions, the child would project an emotional state onto the caregiver for the caregiver to respond to in meeting the needs of the dependent child. Though useful at the time, this method of dealing with needs of the child would become a problem as the child aged and became able to verbalize. At these later dates, others around the child might become confused about what they were experiencing and why, leading to the later, parallel/concordant counter-transference felt by the psychotherapist.

Furthermore, the affects and needs of the young child are known for being intense and unmodulated. If the child grew without changing her method of eliciting responses from others (her objects), an unwary other might suddenly be overtaken by an intense feeling-state to which he or she might respond reflexively, rather than reflectively. As an example, if the child (now physically an adult) felt deprived, she might communicate a loud upset, which could well trigger a squelching response from those around her. Unfortunately, the squelching might be just the type of parental reaction that left the child with unmet needs that arrested her at a certain stage of development, so that, in a tragic type of unconscious repetition compulsion, the patient's original frustration would be repeated over and over again.

In contrast, if the child developed normally, her reactions would be more focused, better modulated, less demanding or compelling, and experienced as less manipulative. The normally developed child might even be able to seek her own gratification independently, or at least to ask for assistance without the other feeling swept away by her needs.

A wider understanding of counter-transference could, of course, be misused by a psychotherapist who lacked the care or discipline to sort out his own conflicts with a patient. In this case, a blind spot or unresolved relational problem in the history of the psychotherapist would be foisted onto the patient, with damaging effects. Used properly, however, a wider understanding of counter-transference could add enormous power to the tools at a psychotherapist's disposal. Now, instead of the psychotherapist feeling shame at becoming bored with a patient, the psychotherapist might wonder if the patient was bored and empty, if the patient was not on track with his real concerns, if the patient was failing to make any empathic connection to the psychotherapist, or a variety of other possibilities. Fantasies or daydreams that might cross the mind of the psychotherapist while listening to the patient now might indicate some deeper unspoken need or condition of the patient rather than simply being a therapeutic lapse.[192]

Turning the new, wider understanding of transference and counter-transference to the subject of therapeutic impasse, the psychotherapist might now have a new way to understand a confusion of roles she found herself in with a particular patient. The psychotherapist might wonder if these roles might represent various split-off unresolved relationship deficiencies that came into play in the therapeutic relationship.[193] Rather than simply reacting instinctively with a deflating or defensive response to the grandiosity or scorn of a patient, the psychotherapist could now "decenter" and analyze her own reactions as further bits of information about the patient, understanding him more quickly or better.

If the treating clinician understood herself rather thoroughly (probably from receiving her own psychotherapy), she could stand confident in the midst of swirling emotions and roles to decipher what the swirl meant. With the help of other cues about the patient's developmental level or actual reports of the patient's history, she could express responses that were more than just reactions—responses that the patient, at his current psychological state, might be able to understand or use to better regulate himself or understand himself more accurately.

In consultation or supervision, the treating psychotherapist with an affect of shame or puzzlement first describes many impasses. When the psychotherapist is ashamed of his reactions or is puzzled, it is difficult for psychotherapy to proceed. When these reactions can be explained as the natural draw of a needy person stuck at a lower developmental level, the psychotherapist can regroup and begin planning responses that are more effective. Some of these responses might indeed be cognitive or behavioral, and some might be psychodynamic, but useful responses seldom, if ever, occur as a knee-jerk reaction or in an atmosphere of confusion or shame. On the other hand, when the needs of the patient are clearly seen, even if the patient is in a very different "spot" from the psychotherapist, and when what is blocking the gratification of those needs is also clearly understood, the psychotherapist will have a variety of interpretive or ameliorating responses that she could make.

---

192   One need only scan the table of contents in Searles' (Ibid.) book (although we recommend reading at least some of the chapters to get the feel for how a therapist might use counter-transference) to get an idea of the multitude of ways in which feeling nuances might be stirred up (without a word) by the patient and thereby brought to the therapist's attention. Giovacchini's book (Ibid.) also contains a variety of examples.

193   Murray (Ibid.) rather severely criticizes this approach, but, we think, unfairly. Used appropriately and with the correct balance between it and the older Freudian understandings of transference and counter-transference (each used correctly with the proper developmental level of transaction), the newer and wider understanding of transference, which Murray variously labels as "two person" or relationship transferences, is appropriate. His complaint is valid, however, if one becomes reductionistic with Object-Relations Theory and thinks of transference and counter-transference *only* in the "external" way, as opposed to the older Freudian "internal" way.

CHAPTER 17

INTERNALIZATIONS:
TRANSMUTING AND THE TRIPARTITE MODEL

Fortunately, we do not have to reinvent the wheel with each new generation. Whether we are considering something as basic as a tool, something more complex such as a strategy or language, or even assemblies of ideas contained in theories and philosophies, we can build on the foundations of our ancestors. We take in their knowledge, imitate it, and improve upon it. Psychological characteristics are no exception. One might observe that the gait or dialect of many members of one family are similar but doubt whether anyone has consciously instructed each member, detail by detail, on ways of carrying oneself or speaking. Bandura talks about how we take in information through observing someone modeling a behavior,[194] and Schafer expands on the subject considerably as it pertains to shape and functioning of the personality.[195]

Specifically, Schafer describes three processes whereby a person's experience with another (object) becomes part of his internal world. The first process, which is typically the most primitive and laden with fantasy, absoluteness, and magic of the world of primary process, is called *incorporation*. In this process, the object is not sensed as a separate being internally, but is experienced as something engulfed or engulfing.[196] In the second process, *introjection*, the represented object is recognized as an internal image—largely, the unmodified perception of the other person (object). The introject related to

---

194 Bandura, A. (1977). Self-efficacy: Toward a unifying theory of behavioral change. *Psychological Review, 84,* 191–215.
195 Schafer, R. (1968). *Aspects of internalization.* New York: International Universities Press (reprinted 1990) and Searles, Ibid., in Chapter 1 of his book.
196 Searles, Ibid., p. 39.

one's impression of himself can serve as a substitute ideal ego, if need be, and both are sorts of internal maps to enable a person to navigate through his relationships and life. The final and most sophisticated process (although it can occur quite early and also be permeated with primary process) is called *identification*. This third type of taking in of another's characteristics changes actual self traits. With many identifications, a person may assimilate or digest different aspects, taking in and assuming some part of the other person's identity and "eliminating" others.

Some theorists suggest that Object-Relations, which are internalized, especially early (pre-Oedipal) Object-Relations, form the basis for the ego, id, and superego of Freud's 1923 tripartite model that most people think of when they think of Freud's theory of human personality functioning.[197] The superego is the best example of the type of thinking thought to contain, particularly in its most immature form, stark representations of authoritative prohibitions of the father against the urges of the id.

Transference and projective identification are two examples of what are considered the results of internalization. In both cases, but extraordinarily in projective identification, the patient's perception of the psychotherapist is colored by her internal objects. As mentioned in the previous chapter, this means that the psychotherapist is likely to quickly feel, in many psychotherapy cases, the nature of the patient's internalized object representations. Some psychotherapists feel so drawn that they actually begin to act in accordance with what would otherwise be alien to them, but familiar to the patient's world of significant others.[198] Awareness of such phenomena associated with the vicissitudes of psychotherapeutic work can help stave off destructive misalliances and enactments.

Kohut sees the role of the psychotherapist who helps as being the provider of the *transmuting internalization*.[199] In the transmuting internalization, the psychotherapist resists the draw of the patient to replicate experiences that have been damaging, deficient, or faulty, instead playing a role that provides the patient with enough of what he needs to form the personality structure that will allow him to leave a developmental stage in

---

197   See St. Clair, M. (2004). "The Freudian Starting Point: Concepts Relevant to Object-Relations and Self-Psychology Theories." In M. St. Clair & J. Wigren, *Object-Relations and self psychology: An introduction* (pp. 1–34). Pacific Grove, CA: Brooks Cole.
        See also Gedo, J. E., & Goldberg, A. (1973). *Models of the mind*. University of Chicago Press (see especially pp. 32–45).

198   This is the negative transference reaction, perhaps first described in Asch, S. (1976). Varieties of negative therapeutic reaction and problems of technique. *Journal of the American Psychoanalytic Association, 24*, 383–407; and then later developed further in Rosenfeld, H. (1978). Notes on the psychopathology and psychoanalytic treatment of some borderline patients. *International Journal of Psycho-Analysis, 59*, 215–221; and further, the subject of an entire book: Seinfeld, J. H. (1990). *The bad object*. Northvale, NJ: Jason Aronson, Inc.

199   Kohut, H. (1984). *How does analysis cure?* University of Chicago Press (see especially pp. 70–71).

which he was arrested and to proceed with maturation without losing coherence as a self. For example, if the patient was not soothed as a very young child, the psychotherapist would model a calm and somewhat soothing attitude so the patient could internalize these qualities or procedures. The psychotherapist is not totally gratifying, in that she "optimally frustrates" so the patient is not eternally dependent upon her but must eventually draw upon his memories of the calm, soothing times with the psychotherapist and reproduce the qualities he observed to calm and soothe himself. If the patient is scattered, perhaps even bordering on disintegration (what the patient might describe as falling apart), the psychotherapist would understand each seemingly errant and unrelated impulse as part of a greater whole self. The psychotherapist might also set limits to prevent the patient from allowing any one part of himself too much headway, as that might upset any fragile balance the patient may have. Again, with optimal frustration, as well as gratification, the patient is eventually able to copy these functions inside and make them part of himself.

Conflicted internalizations, or internalized objects in conflict with the basic needs or designs of the patient, can also create severe problems such as anxiety, guilt, obsessive-compulsive rituals to fend off the anger and guilt about the conflict, and so on. Typically, conflicts are the result of black-and-white thinking and of the patient not seeing alternatives other than victory or surrender for one part or the other. In these cases, the psychotherapist must serve almost as a detective, using transference, counter-transference, history, and what the patient presents to determine what the conflict is about and to find a "third way" out of the logjam. The psychotherapist can help the patient solve the conflict by brainstorming creative resolutions that include the valuable truths contained in both sides of the internal conflict.

In all cases, the psychotherapist uses the relationship for both assessment and cure. Specific psychotherapeutic techniques may be employed (e.g., restatement, reflection, interpretation, and so on), but only after a careful determination of the nature of the problem a patient is facing. What a patient can use—that is, usefully internalize (rather than internalize as a hostile incorporation or introject)—depends on the psychotherapist's accurate understanding of what is missing or needed in the life of the patient. If the psychotherapist sensitively and correctly determines and supplies what is needed, the patient is soon in possession of his own portable coping mechanism that now becomes part of himself. If the psychotherapist, on the other hand, attempts to force an idea (that may even be objectively correct) on the patient that does not fit with the needs of the patient, the psychotherapist may temporarily suppress the symptom, at the expense of the further maturation of the true personality of the person coming to the psychotherapist for help. If the ministrations of the psychotherapist are derivative of a lack of empathic attunement, this may well derive from an intrusion of his or her own counter-transference. This would be an indication that the clinician needs to subject his or her work in the moment with such a patient to self-analysis, consultation with a colleague, and/or exploration in the psychotherapist's *own* personal psychotherapy.

CHAPTER 18

MAKING USE OF TECHNIQUES AND THOUGHT FROM THEORIES OTHER THAN OBJECT-RELATIONS

The example in an earlier chapter about Dr. Normal, who had discovered the wondrous curative powers of penicillin and the many derivative antibiotics created since its discovery, makes a good point: Most ailments require unique treatments. Unfortunately, in the mental health field, we persist in trying to bend the same "medicine" to work for every patient with every ailment coming through the doors of our offices. If our theory is Rogerian, we listen to each patient with great empathy, share with genuineness, and help the patient find out how he really feels, deep down at the center. If our theory is psychodynamic, we search for the constellation of relationships, trauma, and resulting conflicts that caused a set of symptoms to appear, no matter whether the problem is schizophrenia, dysthymia, or fear of flying. It is hoped that, by now, the reader will see the point of the metaphoric story and realize that we are calling for different "medicines"—distinctive treatments for people having problems with diverse diagnostic labels.

Traditional psychoanalysis has long said that people having psychotic conditions or character disorders are not good candidates for psychoanalysis. To understand this, consider for a moment a person with schizophrenia lying on the analytic couch and free-associating with the analyst behind him four times a week. At least three things are wrong with this situation. First, most patients with schizophrenia would not be organized enough to schedule and make four appointments a week. Second, many would find the idea of the analyst being behind and out of sight intolerable. Finally, free-associating would be unlikely to help an already fragmented schizophrenic personality structure.

Psychotic personalities do not need psychoanalysis, Rogerian psychotherapy, Gestalt psychotherapy, or a whole host of other types of therapies. What they need, in summary, is management and containment. That management and containment may include the use of medication, milieu, direction, and education about basic living skills, limit-setting, or any other number of time-honored ways of helping. Severe nonpsychotic depressive personalities need a supportive, empathic, stable, and long-term relationship, perhaps with simultaneous medication, according to the research.[200] According to Giovacchini, as cited in an earlier chapter, and many other authorities, management of depressive personalities, except to prevent suicide, may make the patient worse. Sociopathic personalities benefit from a combination of scrutiny, confrontation, and support; but this patient population does not respect people who simply offer empathy and also uses people who offer analysis to learn new excuses for their behavior.

Each theory (and its accompanying techniques) probably has its place in an integrated psychological approach, depending on the diagnosis (and the attendant developmental stage in question). It may be that a patient who loses control over bowel movements is angry about his parents' marital problems, but starting him off with a psychodynamic or a family-systems approach rarely gets any positive results. This childhood problem (think of it as toilet training) requires a warm, understanding, patient but firm *behavioral* approach, as does the treatment, for example, of fears that are larger than current circumstances warrant (phobias). On the other hand, existential psychotherapy should have many good leads for the psychotherapist to follow when treating a basically healthy person with a life crisis. Cognitive-behavioral approaches often work excellently with the circumscribed problems besetting an otherwise untroubled and healthy person confronted with disorder as a result of an adjustment in life circumstances.

The practice of investigating and finding the right type of intervention for each patient is aided by thinking about the original patient sample treated during the creation

---

200   Antonnuccio, D. O., Danton, W. G., DeNelsky, G. Y., Greenberg, R. P., & Gordon, J .S. (1999). Raising questions about antidepressants. *Psychotherapy and Psychosomatics, 68*(1), 3–14.; Schulberg, H. C., Pilkonis, P. A., & Houck, P. (1998). The severity of major depression and choice of treatment in primary care practice. *Journal of Consulting and Clinical Psychology, 66*(6), 932–938.; American Academy of Child and Adolescent Psychiatry Work Group on Quality Issues—Washington, D.C. (1998). Summary of the practice parameters for the assessment and treatment of children and adolescents with depressive disorders. *Journal of the American Academy of Child and Adolescent Psychiatry, 37*(11), 1234–1238.; and Croghan, T. W., Melfi, C. A., Dobrez, D. G., & Knieser, T. J. (1999). Effect of mental health specialty care on antidepressant length of treatment. *Medical Care, 37*(4), AS20–AS23.

of each theory in relation to the ideas and techniques offered. As common sense would have it, in treating patients like the ones encountered by psychotherapists in their contemporary practices, clinicians typically review research on theoretical and technical perspectives available in the literature. It is especially wise to consider the perspectives of the originators. Patients of today often benefit from the theory and practices that were derived by a gifted psychotherapist from an earlier period who recorded her ideas that were used successfully in ameliorating similar patients' distress. Research has shown that especially gifted psychotherapists may well identify their approach with quite different theoretical labels, but when it comes to treating patients, they are not all that different from one another.

Another method of choosing the correct therapeutic approach is to consider Winnicott's aphorism about good-enough mothering and to ask how a good-enough parent would treat a child having this problem within a particular stage of maturity. If this is coupled with what we have deduced about our patient (through careful diagnosis and an understanding of the developmental etiology of human problems) and carries signs of certain age-appropriate characteristics, it may work well as a therapeutic approach. For example, smearing feces on the wall is probably best stopped by restraint and empathic redirection, whether we are dealing with a child or an adult psychotic. On the other hand, deep discussion with personal sharing probably works best for a mature adult facing a bankruptcy forced by illness. Later generations of psychotherapists need to develop sound conceptual methodologies that enable them to identify essential psychodynamics and characteristics to apply particular treatment methodologies correctly.

CHAPTER 19

MANAGED CARE AND SHORT-TERM, CRISIS, AND INPATIENT TREATMENT

O bject-Relations and Self-Psychology often are required as theories for use with patients in long-term psychotherapy. This is probably because of their association with psychoanalysis and also because they are derived from successful work with deeply disturbed people whose very personality structures are in need of reworking. These two theories often are applied to cases in which either short-term or long-term psychotherapy is indicated.

As suggested in previous chapters, accurate diagnosis according to the developmental model is important for selecting the correct treatment. Problems that come up in basically mentally healthy people with sound development tend to be more circumscribed and crisis-oriented. The correct treatment in these cases, therefore, is not long-term but short-term, problem-oriented psychotherapy. If the person is suffering from a more pervasive problem such as Borderline Personality Disorder or major depression, the research suggests that long-term psychotherapy is indicated.[201] In these cases, cost savings obtained by forcing the patient into short-term psychotherapy are offset by increased medical costs, lost productivity and wages, and greater use of other social services.[202]

---

201 See Seligman, M. (1995). Does therapy help? *Consumer Reports, November,* 734–739.; Blatt, S. (1992). The differential effect of psychotherapy and psychoanalysis on anaclitic and introjective patients: The Menninger Psychotherapy Research Project revisited. *Journal of the American Psychoanalytic Association, 40,* 691–724; and Blatt, S., & Ford, R. (1994). *Therapeutic change: An Object-Relations perspective.* New York: Plenum Press.

202 See the second page of the article "Mental Health Services to Cut Overall Health Costs," in *Psychology's Role in Healthcare* (1994), published by the American Psychological Association in Washington, D.C., which cited studies showing (1) markedly increased use of physician services among 20,000 Columbia Medical Plan participants when persons with mental illness did not receive treatment for their conditions, (2) that Bell South's claims in the

Some managed care organizations (MCOs) and case managers may attempt to force all psychotherapy into the short-term mode, no matter what. This is done either out of limited training, indoctrination, or selfish submission to one side of a built-in conflict of interest (case managers and their companies earn greater profits and bonuses through denying care, regardless of the reason). In the long term, legislation and litigation will probably reduce or eliminate these conflicts of interest. The public will eventually grow aware of the impacts that managed care decisions have on the outcome of health treatments and will learn that health insurance premium monies have been diverted into companies' and managers' profits. Of course, not all MCOs, and certainly not all case managers, are selfish or blind; many of them realize that different patients require different levels of care and authorize accordingly.

There are also occasions when a patient who ideally needs long-term care can also benefit from targeted short-term interventions. Again, using insights obtained from Object-Relations Theory, one can see that treatment, even of the seriously disturbed, is composed of many stages. For many patients, the first stage may simply be to build a trusting working alliance. This might be done with a variety of tools, including good listening and helping the patient solve the problem he originally presents. Although this problem might be only a symptom of a much larger structural problem, in the interests of recognizing the patient's autonomy (for reality-based reasons or for other causes), the treatment might stop at this point. For the time being, with an honest acknowledgment on the part of the clinician to the patient, other issues will probably eventually need to be resolved.

In this last instance, when short-term psychotherapy is offered for a diagnosis in which long-term psychotherapy is indicated, the psychotherapist will need to work especially hard at maintaining good clinical ethics and at facing the professional challenge brought to him. On occasion, this may involve finding creative solutions (sometimes with the help of case managers in MCOs) so that the long-term psychotherapy necessary can be offered.

1980s and 1990s mental health dropped six million dollars when they adopted the least-restrictive policies for psychological services, (3) that McDonnell Douglas saw both a 50% decrease in psychiatric inpatient use and a 34% decrease in per capita mental health expense when they removed the limits on their mental health coverage and reduced costs to the policy holder, (4) that ten thousand Aetna beneficiaries dropped their medical expenses progressively in the three years following the inclusion of a mental health benefit, and (5) that other studies are also mentioned.

A recent meta-analysis has concluded that the addition of behavioral health services, "particularly when delivered as part of primary medical care" (p. 290) can be integral to the overall health enhancement of the population. This interesting overview is referenced in Blount, A., Schoenbaum, M., Kathol, R., Rollman, B. L., Thomas, M., O'Donohue, W., & Peek, C. J. (2007). The economics of behavioral health services in medical settings: A summary of the evidence. *Professional Psychology: Research and Practice, 38*(3), 290–297.

Inpatient treatment has never been the first avenue of treatment for psychoanalysts (in fact, historically, it was sometimes found to be offered only by other psychiatrists). Ignorance, therefore, is the only reason for assuming that any psychodynamic theory (which usually has a strong focus on the relationship) is likely to lead to longer hospitalizations. In psychodynamic group practice, for example, where many of us provide similar psychotherapy approaches, only 1.1% of our patients were hospitalized during 1995, for a total of only 33 days, figures that are quite low, even in this day of managed care. Our belief is that the reason for the infrequent and short-term use of inpatient treatment by those using Object-Relations Theory and Self-Psychology is that the relationship, rather than the hospital, is, in many cases, sufficient to hold the patient. Psychotherapists using these new theories are especially prone to focus quite early on establishing a relationship. If they are good, they will, without necessarily even stating it, engender feelings of trust and hope that are often enough (with sometimes the additional help of psychopharmacology) to treat a person successfully without resorting to intensive inpatient treatment. Of course, this will not always work, and patients will need to be protected against harming themselves or others, or simply need to be contained in a more physical sense. A review of the literature, however, quickly shows that the clinical anecdote being offered above, about the authors' own group practices, is typical of the field; the case illustrations are almost exclusively about outpatient treatment. If this data were included in the analyses done by managed care personnel, perhaps they would be more friendly to people using these new relationship-oriented therapies (though eclectic in practice, they have strong theoretical underpinnings).

In summary, it is important to realize that neither Object-Relations Theory nor Self-Psychology dictate long-term psychotherapy solutions for all patients with any variety of problems (unlike the notorious Dr. Normal of the previous chapter). Diagnosis, etiology, and even research will provide the best indicators of the types of treatment necessary and of the approximate typical lengths of time required. Reality factors may intrude, however, and the ethical clinician must do his best to see that the intrusion is minimal for the patient to receive the type of care she needs to properly recover.

CHAPTER 20

WHAT DOES THE RESEARCH SAY?

As was noted in the beginning of this book, psychoanalysis is not only a form of treatment for disturbed mental states but also a theory of personality and psychological principles. Furthermore, psychoanalysis is a research methodology as originally conceived by Freud, who was principally trying to understand the workings of the mind and outline laws by which seemingly illogical, random behaviors and symptoms could be understood as making *psycho*-logical sense. Psychoanalysis as a curative treatment was only a fortunate result of his investigative method for analyzing the workings of the mind. His numerous case studies, historically seen as the primary conveyors of new knowledge in psychiatry and medicine, were incorporated into the new discipline.

Freud's most famous cases have been the subject of intensive study and debates since they were first presented and include the case of Hans, a five-year-old boy who developed a phobia after seeing a horse fall down in the street. This case analysis, actually conducted by the boy's father, who was a pupil of Freud's, was instrumental in developing the theory of the Oedipal phase of development.[203] Freud's earlier work with Joseph Breuer, which marked the beginning of psychoanalysis [with the publication of *Studies in Hysteria* (1895)], described the traumatic roots of hysteria and, by extension, other mental disorders. Although Freud worked with a variety of patients manifesting a broad range of symptomatology, hysteria was a very common disorder at that time and even found its way into the discussion of one of his treatment failures. This is the case of Dora, a teenager he treated briefly before she abruptly terminated (as a testament to Freud, he assumed that others, like himself, could

---

203   Freud, S. (1909). *Analysis of a phobia in a five-year-old boy*. The standard edition of the complete psychological works of Sigmund Freud (Vol. 10). New York: W. W. Norton.

learn from not only their successes but also their failures).[204] Although Breuer's treatment of Anna O. in *Studies in Hysteria* showed the power of transference (unrecognized by Breuer, who broke off the treatment when the patient developed an intense, erotic tie to him, complete with a false pregnancy), Freud's treatment of Dora seems to have suffered from his lack of attention to his own negative counter-transference, which developed in relation to his willful and rebellious adolescent patient.

By far, the most famous of Freud's cases were his successful treatment and cure of the so-called "Rat Man" (referred to as such by virtue of his rat obsession, among many others) and the "Wolf Man" (his pseudonym derived from the famous dream he reported to Freud, which is analyzed exhaustively in the case study).[205] Both cases explored the *childhood* origins of neurosis and detailed the role of infantile sexuality in their etiology. Both cases also detailed Freud's work with the transference and his interpretation of this psychoanalytical artifact as a core to the effective outcome of a psychotherapeutic treatment.

Psychoanalytical journals continue to publish new case studies as psychoanalysts seek to confirm, extend, or disconfirm certain elements of psychoanalytical theory and technique. An arc of tension exists over the different types of investigation employed between psychoanalysts and behaviorists/cognitive-behaviorists. In contrast to the former, the latter have felt that experimentally driven research designs are the only proper methodologies for analyzing human behavior. Research design is precisely the problem, argue psychoanalysts, who see the designs as narrow and reductionistic, associated with quantitative, experimental research and questions. The experimental results of "rat psychology" research lacks relevance for the complexities and nuances of human subjects and patients, with a limited ability to generalize the obtained experimental results to real-world functioning. By focusing on only small, observable behavioral units, the research distorts the subject of study into a reactive *object*: It encodes a distinct bias in that it rules out any possibility of unconscious process, including the elements of conscious but nonverbalized thought, feeling, and intentionality. Psychoanalysis, with its focus on variables that cannot be directly observed (and therefore seen as being incapable of being proved *or* disproved), has been scorned as being a pseudo-science. Happily, some modicum of rapprochement has been achieved with the demise of so-called radical

---

204   Freud, S. (1905). *Fragment of an analysis of a case of hysteria*. The standard edition of the complete psychological works of Sigmund Freud (Vol. 7). New York: W. W. Norton.
205   For the "Rat Man," see Freud, S. (1909). *Notes upon a case of obsessional neurosis*. The standard edition of the complete psychological works of Sigmund Freud (Vol. 10). New York: W. W. Norton. For the "Wolf Man," see Freud, S. (1918). *From the history of an infantile neurosis*. The standard edition of the complete psychological works of Sigmund Freud (Vol. 17). New York: W. W. Norton.

behaviorism, in favor of cognitive-behavioral perspectives that give credence to some mental activities of the mind, such as thinking and feeling (and *very* reassuring to now have agreement that people think and feel and that these internal activities can affect our intentions and behaviors!). It is also interesting to note that two leading proponents of the research and cognitive-behavioral perspectives (Aron T. Beck and Albert Ellis) have backgrounds as psychoanalysts.

Recently, Blampied noted that the case study method might be augmented by single-case designs. The former "are descriptive and normally cannot support valid inferences," or so Blampied asserts, whereas the latter "are controlled experiments" that permit valid inferences.[206] He notes that greater inclusion of such single-case research, as it focuses on the individual, may have greater relevance for the pragmatic applications often necessary in clinical psychology and clinical psychoanalysis. Certainly, a greater interest in qualitative research studies, *à la* Mahler's work noted above, shows a widening of psychology's perspective on what constitutes research.[207]

To return to psychoanalysis proper, the central tenet that processes exist outside of conscious awareness remains the bedrock for any theory purporting to call itself psychoanalytical. Westen is one author who examines such matters as memory, affective processes, the neurological basis for unconscious emotional responses, and defensive processes. Much as Aldous Huxley wrote in *Doors of Perception*, Westen posits the necessity of a filter, without terming the unconscious as such, that permits us to separate essential from nonessential detail and, therefore, concentrate and act with some coherence. In short, "something" must be at work to enable us to focus on the task at hand; if not, we would have to consciously try to sort out and screen, prioritize, and reject a number of competing stimuli and agendas.[208] For example, I would have to consciously reassemble for myself how to translate my emergent thoughts into words and their constituent parts, including the spelling and meanings of the words, as they tumble out on to the page. But how could this be accomplished if I were aware, moment to moment, of the pressure of my body against the chair, clothing against skin, sounds both inside and outside of the building, the subtleties of my musculature working to maintain my posture, or the focusing of my eyesight to the task at hand—let alone distractions of the memories or

---

206   See Blampied, N. M. (2000). Single-case research designs: A neglected alternative. *American Psychologists,* 55(8), 960.
207   Mahler, M., Pine, F., & Bergman, A. (1975). *The psychological birth of the human infant.* New York: Basic Books.
208   Westen, D. (1998). Unconscious thought, feeling, and motivation: The end of a century-long debate. In R. F. Bornstein, & J. M. Masling (Eds.), *Empirical perspectives on the psychoanalytical unconscious.* Washington, D.C.: American Psychological Association.

associations that writing may invoke in me. It is clear that anyone would collapse before a single word had been written!

Confirmation of the unconscious is present across a variety of the cognitive and neurosciences, as well as the more traditionally psychological. Citing the case of H. M., who underwent very drastic neurosurgery to control his seizures, Milner et al. found that with the destruction of the neural pathways in the hippocampus, the conscious retrieval of newly learned information and experiences was lost.[209] For example, in spite of working with Dr. Milner across twenty years, H. M. was never able to recognize her face; nevertheless, he continued to learn. He acquired the ability to write upside down, albeit without any recognition that he had ever performed the task. On a more affective level, following a visit to his mother in the hospital, although unable to recall anything of the visit, he entertained the vague sense that something was wrong with his mother.[210] Westen reasoned that this was possible because "affective knowledge . . . involved associative learning—forming a new association between his mother and a feeling—which, like semantic priming, involved automatic activation of unconscious networks of association."[211] Similarly, we know that children appear to automatically pick up the grammatical rules of the culture into which they are born. The automaticity of such unconscious processes is clearly an adaptive advantage. Much like the earlier example of the hyper-reflective writer, evolution clearly would favor a species that could rely on learning derived from experience and thus be able to discriminate the important aspects of particular stimuli and produce efficient responses in relation to novel, similar, or identical contexts.

Defensive processes and specific defense mechanisms that protect the self from the displeasure associated with negative affective experiences such as anxiety and guilt have been discussed in this book. These defense mechanisms, it is hypothesized, are unconscious elements of the ego that assist psychical regulation. Extrapolating from adult attachment research, Westen and Ainsworth suggest that early relational patterns established with the mother continue to manifest themselves across the lifespan.[212] Here, Westen draws on the seminal work of Ainsworth and her colleagues in a series of experiments employing what Ainsworth termed the "strange situation." In brief, this experimental design consisted of babies (from 50 to 52 weeks old) being taken with their mothers to an unfamiliar room

---

209   Milner, B., Corkin, S., & Teuber, H. L. (1968). Further analysis of the hippocampal amnesiac syndrome: Fourteen-year follow-up study of H. M. *Neuropsychologia, 6*, 215–234.

210   Cited in Westen, D. (1998). Ibid.

211   Ibid., pg. 9.

212   Ibid. See also Ainsworth, M. D. S., Blehan, M. C., Waters, E., & Wall, S. (1978). *Patterns of attachment: A psychological study of the strange situation.* Hillsdale, NJ: Erlbaum.; and Ainsworth, M. D. S. (1985). I: Pattern of infant-mother attachment: Antecedents and effects on development. II: Attachments across the life span. *Bulletin of the New York Academy of Medicine, 6*, 771–812.

and left on their own, intermittently, with their mothers' occasional departure. The babies were free to explore and to play with toys that were available. At some point, a stranger entered the room and, after a brief interval, the mother left. The baby's reaction to the departure was noted. The mother returned, re-engaged with the baby and, after the stranger exited the room, left again. This was followed closely by the reappearance of the stranger and, after another short interval, the mother's return.

From these studies, Ainsworth and colleagues established three types of attachment.[213] A secure attachment (Group B) was evidenced by some minor upset during the separation from mother but comfort upon her return. Those babies also engaged in exploratory play. More pathological reactions related to disturbances in the mother-infant bond were termed anxious/avoidant attachment (Group A) and ambivalent attachment (Group C).

Group A infants displayed little or no distress during the periods of their mothers' departure. They *avoided* the mother during her return (while avoiding the stranger less) and displayed a precocious independence that had a pseudo-autonomous quality to it. They seemed to find the toys more compelling than human connectedness. Their expressions of anger seemed to come at odd and inappropriate times.

Some infants displayed an ambivalent attachment (Group C) and were the most overtly disturbed. They displayed apprehension and distress even before the mother's departure, were inhibited in their exploration of the room, and were unable to engage in independent play. They were also fearful of the stranger and became extremely distressed during separation from their mothers. Even reunions with the mother seemed conflicted for them, as they veered between rejecting and clinging behavior.

Perhaps not surprisingly, Ainsworth and colleagues suggested a relationship between the type of attachment observed and the type of parenting delivered.[214] Thus, Group C babies may have been responded to in ways that seemed capricious—whether attentive or rejecting—in unpredictable and, hence, indecipherable ways for the baby. Kumin reports that Main and Westen indicated that the Group A infant's behavior is "highly correlated with the three qualities of their mother's behavior towards them: the mother's aversion to physical contact, her angry and threatening behavior, and her restriction of emotional expressiveness."[215] In this respect, confirmatory information is arising from research not

213   Ibid.
214   Ibid.
215   Kumin, I. (1996). *Pre-object relatedness: Early attachment and the psychoanalytic situation*. New York: Guilford Press (p. 140). See also Main, M., & Westen, D. (1982). Avoidance of the attachment figure in infancy: Descriptions and interpretations. In C. M. Parks & H. Stevenson (Eds.), *The place of attachment in human behavior*. New York: Basic Books.

specific to the psychoanalytical field, nor necessarily focused principally on attachment theory. One such study[216] examined children whose development has been compromised by virtue of a number of environmental impingements or developmental traumata proceeding from such things as poverty and exposure to violence, which, contextually, would put children at risk for developing psychopathology. Masten's research would suggest that resilience is far more common and less extraordinary than one would be inclined to believe at first blush.

Significantly, Masten isolates a rather narrowed list of factors that associated with productive adaptation. This is very positive and holds out great hope not only for children, but ultimately society, inasmuch as extraordinary measures are not necessarily required but that more *ordinary* resources available to assist adaptation and associated systems (for example, the family) may be sufficient, given the proper qualitative elements. Indeed, Masten goes on to note that the factors include "connections to competent and caring adults, family, and a community, cognitive and self-regulation skills, positive views of self, and motivation to be effective in the environment . . . Across different situations and research strategies, the consistent support for these resources suggests that basic human adaptational systems are at work, many of which have been studied in depth under the rubric of constructs such as attachment, authoritative parenting, intelligence, self-regulation, self-efficacy, pleasure-in-mastery, or intrinsic motivation."[217] Such research on adaptation as increasingly being developed within the psychoanalytical community, therefore, are being replicated by other developmental psychologists with somewhat differing perspectives and orientations.

Bowlby's notion of internal working models (IWMs) and Stern's representations of interactions that have become generalized (RIGs) suggest that early constituent elements and routines that constitute relationships at a most basic level (including the parents' attunements and accurate "matching" of their babies' need states) become the templates of object-relationships. Expectations based on such experiences with caregivers may be colored by accompanying affects and emotions. These may form one of the templates for a concept important not only to classical psychoanalytical theory but also to Object-Relations theories in general, for the processes of introjection, displacement, and projection: namely, *transference*.[218] The research of Main and Weston and of Main,

216   Masten, A. S. (2001). Ordinary magic: Resilience processes in development. *American Psychologist, 56*(3), 227–238.
217   Masten, A. S. (2001). Ibid., p. 234.
218   Bowlby, J. (1982). *Attachment and loss: Volume three—Loss.* New York: Basic Books.; and Stern, D. (1985). *The interpersonal world of the infant.* New York: Basic Books. See also Slade, A., & Aber, J. L. (1992).

Kaplan, and Cassidy suggests that how one was parented will partially determine the type of parent one becomes—producing a kind of intergenerational transmission of relative health or psychopathology.[219] Studies suggest that this outcome is far from conscious. Weston reports on research with avoidant adults:

> Avoidant adults, like avoidant infants, are hypothesized to shut-off or deactivate attachment-related feelings as a way of coping with them. In fact, the more individuals showed deactivating strategies by disavowing feelings, the more physiological reactivity they manifested while answering affectively evocative questions about separations, rejections, and parental threats. This disjunction between reported concerns and physiologically expressed affect appeared only while participants were responding to probes that were theoretically expected to draw this kind of defensive strategies (*e.g.*, rejections) and did not emerge on affectedly neutral items.[220]

Self-report is commonsensically considered to have dubious validity. Wittingly or not, we often try to accentuate the positive and minimize the negative. Nevertheless, it is the experience of many clinicians that the opposite may be seen at times in the professional setting; in other words, observed reactions go against the grain of social desirability, such as may be the case in malingering. For example, an individual may report being far worse off than he really is, as demonstrated by various physiological or psychological measures, to receive disability benefits or avoid criminal prosecution. Studies of individuals who reported to researchers a relatively healthy psychological history and makeup, yet had more emotionally disturbed backgrounds as assessed by their discussion of early memories, showed greater physiological signs of anxiety during mildly stressful, experimentally controlled tasks (e.g., reading aloud) while "declaring themselves to be the *least* anxious during these tasks."[221] Presumably, this is emblematic of defense mechanisms in operation outside of conscious awareness.

Attachments, drives, and development: Conflicts and convergences in theory. In J. W. Barron, M. N. Eagle, & D. L. Wolitzky (Eds.), *Interface of psychoanalysis and psychology*. Washington, DC: American Psychological Association.
219 Main and Westen, Ibid.; Westen, D. (1998).; and Main, M., Kaplan, N., & Cassidy, J. (1985). Security in infancy, childhood, and adulthood: A move to the level of representation. In I. Bretherton & E. Waters (Eds.), *Growing points of attachment theory and research*. Monographs of the Society for Research and Child Development, 50(1–2), 67–104. Cited in Westen, D. (1998), Ibid.
220 Westen, D. (1998). Ibid., pg. 26.
221 Dozier, M., & Koback, R. (1992). Psychophysiology and attachment interviews: Converging evidence for deactivating strategies. *Child Development, 63*, 1473–1480. (Cited in Westen, D., Ibid., p. 26.) See also Schedler, J., Mayman, M., & Mannis, M. (1993). The illusion of mental health. *American Psychologists, 48*, 1117–1131. (Cited in Westen, D. (1998). Ibid. p. 27.)

The centrality of a holding, containing, soothing, and regulatory attachment with the mother is clearly a central tenet of psychoanalytical thought—not only in reference to optimal development itself but also in understanding child or adult psychopathology that may manifest itself initially with early warning signs and more explicitly later in the lifespan. Freud discussed the particular psychological meanings of such a bond, aside from the more purely biologically driven elements:

> Anxiety is seen to be a product of the infant's mental helplessness, which is a natural counterpart of its biological helplessness. The striking coincidence by which the anxiety of the new-born baby and the anxiety of the infant in arms are both conditioned by separation from the mother does not need to be explained on psychological lines. It can be accounted for simply in biology; for, just as the mother originally satisfied the needs of the foetus through the apparatus of her own body, so now, after its birth she continues to do so although partly by other means. There is much more continuity between the intra-uterine life and earliest infancy then the impressive caesura of birth would have us believe. What happens is that the child's biological situation as a foetus is replaced by a *psychical object-relation to its mother* [emphasis added].[222]

In this respect, it is intriguing to consider the question of how this early, primary object-relations unit becomes introjected and maintained across time in the unconscious psyche of the adult. As was noted above, affective elements of the attachment appear to persist beyond childhood. Can the soothing and regulatory functions of the mother—her accurate-enough *anticipation* of, let alone *active, responsive* orientation to her infant's or child's need states—be encoded in the unconscious? What can remain so encoded in the mind over a lifespan, and yet be born from this wordless time before symbols were available to the infant for knowing and therefore for conceivably coherent remembering? What are the mechanisms by which such soothing, preverbal experiences are able to become part of the self and remain available for subsequent self-soothing, calming, and drive regulation in the physical absence of the mothering one, and at chronological points in time further and further from their origins? Perhaps we are all, in fact, forever in search of this original, symbiotic bond. Perhaps in each of us—to varying degrees, and owing to our unique histories—it must be re-evoked, re-experienced, and re-fueled, however indirectly or derivatively (and hence, unrecognized for what it really is). A great premium

---

222   Freud, S. (1926). *Inhibitions, symptoms, and anxiety.* The standard edition of the complete psychological works of Sigmund Freud (Vol. 20). New York: W. W. Norton. (Cited in Kumin, I., (1996), pp. 12 and 128.)

has been placed in Western capitalist-industrialist societies on individuality, autonomous functioning, and separateness. At times, this seems to minimize the importance of collective, communal concerns and the explicit and implicit social contracts that provide the impetus for societies to coalesce and function. Many individuals may seek to *diminish* the felt sense of separateness by "belonging" to a significant other as part of a couple or to establish themselves as a member of a family.

Toward the end of diminishing feelings of separateness, some researchers are exploring the interface between more-or-less autonomous functioning and self-in-relation competencies. Drawing heavily from psychoanalytical Object-Relations theories, Clark and Ladd[223] look at the interplay between the quality of the bond between parent and child and the relationship to the children's competencies regarding forming friendships, the degree of acceptance from peers, and prosocial orientations. The authors found that more-secure connectedness with parents facilitated, in a positive direction, the child's securing mutual friendships and acceptance by peers. The authors speculate that "through connected interactions with parents, children develop an empathic socio-emotional orientation that serves as a foundation for interpreting social situations and responding prosocially to age-mates. This prosocial-empathic orientation, and the actions that are predicated upon it, encourage peers to see children as desirable relational partners."[224] The children may even attempt to address, however unconsciously, the more-or-less adaptive and maladaptive elements of their own experiences of being parented and belonging to a family. Although it may seem incomprehensible to some that *all* elements of our selves-in-relation-to-the-world are at least partially governed by such archaic strivings, a number of psychoanalysts have recently turned their attention to the psychological functions and meanings of employer-employee relations and belonging to organizations or nation-states.[225]

We could also examine elements of religious experiences, mystical states, and substance-induced alterations in consciousness, artistic creativity, and sexual experiences through a similar lens, wherein the boundaries between self and other are experienced as becoming more fluid and blurred. Of course, Freud himself also wrote extensively on

---

223   Clark, K. E., & Ladd, G. W. (2000). Connectedness and autonomy support in parent-child relationships: Links to children's socio-emotional orientation and peer relationships. *Development Psychology, 36*(4), 485–498.
224   Clark, K. E., & Ladd, G. W. (2000). Ibid., p. 495.
225   See, for example, Czander, W. M. (1993). *The psychodynamics of work and organizations.* New York: Guilford Press.; Diamond, M. A. (1993). *The unconscious life of organizations.* Westport, CT: Quorum Books.; Kets de Vries, M. F. R. (Ed.). (1984). *The irrational executive: Psychoanalytic explorations in management.* New York: International Universities Press.; Stapley, L. (1996). *The personality of the organisation: A psychodynamic explanation of culture and change.* London: Free Association Books.; Volkan, V. D. (1988). *The need to have enemies and allies: From clinical practice to international relationships.* Northvale, NJ: Jason Aronson Inc.; and Wallace, A. F. C. (1970). *Culture and personality.* New York: Random House.

cultural phenomena and profoundly influenced sociological and anthropological theory and researchers (such as the sociologist Talcott Parsons).[226]

Therefore, it is somewhat surprising, given what has been elucidated up to this point, that there should exist, *seemingly* in complete opposition from the apparent need for separation, discourse exemplified by some psychoanalytical researchers in articulating a complementary focus. They have posited what they term a *Oneness Motif,* which is defined as a "drive to become part of, at one with, or belong[ing] to, a larger whole."[227] Lloyd H. Silverman is the researcher most closely associated with originating the legacy of psychoanalytically grounded research using subliminal tachistoscopic stimulation (rapid projection of images or words), in what he termed subliminal psychodynamic activation, or SPA.[228] SPA presented research subjects with certain phrases through the tachistoscope, presenting stimuli to its subjects at a level beyond (or beneath) their capacity to consciously apprehend it. Such research has variously attempted to elicit defensive, compensatory, or dysfunctional responses by evoking conflicts hypothesized by psychoanalytical theorists. It has been designed, as well, to bring out more purely adaptive responses associated with the fantasy of oneness that can offset those hypothesized disruptive forces. In research done with relatively high-functioning people who had schizophrenia, Silverman discusses the change of the stimulus "Mommy and I are One" to "I am Mommy."[229] He notes that the latter phrase elicited psychopathological reactions and speculated that this was because of the connotations of engulfment and the consequent loss of the self; thus, not *all* merger fantasies may be gratifying. A great deal depends on one's personality organization.

Another trend in research explores the enhancing or soothing properties of subliminally activated fantasies. Sometimes, "Mommy and I are One" was used in one experimental condition, with the neutral control message "People are Walking" for another subject pool. Siegel and Weinberger report fairly consistent findings that psychotherapy session effectiveness, enhancement of academic performance, and enhancement of mood were all positively influenced when, prior to the performance of some task, subjects were

226   Freud, S. (1913). *Totem and taboo.* The standard edition of the complete psychological works of Sigmund Freud (Vol. 13). New York: W. W. Norton.; Freud, S. (1927). *The future of an illusion.* The standard edition of the complete psychological works of Sigmund Freud (Vol. 21). New York: W. W. Norton.; and Freud, S. (1930). *Civilization and its discontents.* The standard edition of the complete psychological works of Sigmund Freud (Vol. 21). New York: W. W. Norton.

227   For examples, see Siegel, P., & Weinberger, J. (1998). *Capturing the "mommy and I are one" merger fantasy: The oneness motif.* In R. F. Bornstein & J. M. Masling (Eds.), Ibid., p. 72.

228   Silverman, L. H. (1983). The subliminal psychodynamic activation method: Overview and comprehensive listing of studies. In J. M. Masling (Ed.), *Empirical studies of psychoanalytical theories* (Vol. 1). Hillsdale, NJ: The Analytic Press.

229   Ibid.

exposed to the "Mommy and I are One" stimulus, as opposed to "People are Walking."[230] These experiments were extended to other studies, in which the subliminal message "Mommy is Gone" was presented in an attempt to rule out the possibility that the former results may have been due to the subject latching on to the word "Mommy." In the latter experiment, the "Mommy and I are One" group scored highest in regard to positive affect (that is, nondysphoric), with the "Mommy is Gone" group scoring the lowest. "People are Walking" groups scored in the middle.[231] Silverman, on the basis of his cumulative analysis of the studies that he and his colleagues inspired, makes a number of cautionary advisories.[232] For example, a Virginia researcher had failed to replicate the findings with subjects who had schizophrenia. In conversations with one of the psychologists supervising the study, she noted that, in the case of many *Southern* subjects with schizophrenia, the word or the term "Mama" is more normative when referring to their mothers, so "Mommy" may have lacked an important evocative meaning for these subjects. The relatively positive or negative connotations surrounding "Mommy and I are One" may indeed be related to a type or degree of psychopathology, as suggested in the above research, as opposed to the reactions of more "neurotic" and well-integrated subjects.

Finally, Silverman articulated a response that addressed not only some of the individual and/or group differences obtained but that also addresses some of the questions brought up earlier in this chapter. His findings certainly raise the possibility of the existence, if you will, of an internalized mother, including a representation of the total aggregate of maternal care and "holding" (*à la* Winnicott) that constituted "Mother" in our earliest, pre-symbolic experiences of Her—and that is a stand-in for an actual Her—that persists into adulthood. The soothing, calming, positive effects of exposure to such subliminal stimuli necessitate a recognition of the unconscious existence of an internalization of the experienced all-good mother of infancy and childhood—that is, the remembrance of a satisfying, loving, and calming caregiver.[233]

With reference to research on psychoanalytical treatment approaches, Jones discusses some of his work as a psychoanalyst, professor of psychology, and Director of the Berkeley Psychotherapy Research Project.[234] Jones and his colleagues analyzed

---

230   Siegel & Weinberger (1998). Ibid.
231   Ibid.
232   Silverman, L. H. (1983). Ibid.
233   Ibid.
234   Jones, E. E. (2000). Evidence for a new theory of therapeutic action. *Psychologist-Psychoanalyst, 21*(2), 14–18. See also his new book on the subject of devising new strategies for investigating the process and efficacy of psychoanalytical psychotherapy: Jones, E. E. (2000). *Therapeutic action: A guide to psychoanalytic therapy.* Northvale, NJ: Jason Aronson, Inc.

videotapes and complete transcripts of sessions of psychoanalytical psychotherapy and psychoanalysis in a quantitative single-case research design. Progress and change across very extended periods, at regular intervals, could be explored, uniquely, for each patient. The participation and influence of the psychotherapist also could be addressed so that the complexity of the change process could be more adequately assessed. By examining the patient-therapist interaction structures, Jones rendered very nuanced, idiosyncratic data open to investigation and consensual verification by other, independent investigators.

Addressing some of the anti-psychoanalytical bias in the culture at large noted elsewhere in this volume, Gunderson and Gabbard[235] and Freedman, Hoffenberg, Vorus, and Frosch[236] address the relevance and efficacy of psychoanalytic psychotherapy and treatment, in general. These authors also note the need to engage in ongoing research, albeit relevant to the psychoanalytical enterprise, to rebut the attempts to undermine the legitimacy of psychoanalysis and claim the mantel of authority and (unique) effectiveness implied by such terms as empirically supported treatment or evidence-based treatment— euphemistic code for behavioristic or cognitive-behavioristic theory and technique. Too often, such research is constructed in artificial ways to address a narrow, symptomatic expression (for example, a discreet behavior) and institutes a programmed, manualized intervention protocol, and the nuanced, rich, complex, and highly variable nature of actual clinical practice of unique, real clinicians when faced with the requirements posed by the need to appropriately treat their real, unique patients across a variety of organized healthcare settings is lost.

The proponents of manualized treatments, however, have taken the high ground, marginalizing psychoanalysis and calling into question not only its effectiveness but its very essence as a valid set of theories and, by extension, an ethical treatment method that should be applied to clinical populations and various psychopathological syndromes. Third-party payors and pharmaceutical companies, which have enormous vested interests in eradicating longer-term, *psychological* treatment approaches such as psychoanalysis, have enthusiastically endorsed an anti-psychoanalytical bias and, in the case of pharmaceutical concerns, supporting research that purports to demonstrate a clear advantage of medication-based care over psychological treatment.

---

235   Gunderson, J. G., & Gabbard, G. O. (1999). Making the case for psychoanalytic therapies in the current psychiatric environment. *Journal of the American Psychoanalytic Association, 47*(3), 679–704.; and Pole, N. (2000). Making the case for single-case research. *Psychologist-Psychoanalyst, 21*(2), 19–21.

236   Freedman, N., Hoffenberg, J. D., Vorus, N., & Frosch, A. (1999). The effectiveness of psychoanalytic psychotherapy: The role of treatment duration, frequency of sessions, and the therapeutic relationship. *Journal of the American Psychoanalytic Association, 47*(3), 741–772.

An earlier study by Karon and VandenBos,[237] citing the Michigan State Psychotherapy Research Project, showed a clear advantage of *psychoanalytical* psychotherapy over other modes of psychotherapy, medication, or medication and psychotherapy, even when treating more severe types of psychopathology. These studies are even more remarkable given the ostensible admonitions against employing psychoanalytical treatments with more-severe psychopathology and with fewer so-called psychologically minded patients. The subjects for this research project were generally inner-city, poor, and often African-American patients. Freedman and colleagues[238] note that in their varied sample of patients at a low-fee psychoanalytical clinic and in their meta-analyses of other studies, therapeutic gains were observed to increase with length of stay, from 6 to 32 months. Treatment gains were further supported by greater frequency. Patients in twice-weekly psychotherapy did better than patients with once-weekly treatment, and those in thrice-weekly psychotherapy made even more gains than those in twice-weekly treatment. The greater the frequency, the more significant the therapeutic progress and the more lasting the gains were across time. These findings were especially significant regarding increased frequency for patients self-described as anxious or suffering from an eating disorder. The overall length or duration of treatment was significant for patients presenting with concerns relating to family disorganization and stress.

The authors of this book certainly support the growing trend to subject psychoanalytical principles and treatment methodologies to empirical research. This research to date has demonstrated the efficacy of short- and long-term psychoanalytical treatment. Worthy of note is that this efficacy is extended beyond the so-called worried well that is so often disparagingly accorded to psychoanalytical treatments, as, again, psychotically disorganized and characterologically disturbed patients also have shown clear benefit from psychoanalytic treatment. We would also hope that the practitioners and practitioners-to-be reading this book develop their own "databases" and think scientifically regarding the work they are doing in their clinical practices. As Pole[239] notes, professionals practicing in the field are uniquely qualified and positioned to undertake such ongoing research and contribute to the growing body of literature. With the new theoretical paradigms emerging, including the one in this volume, and the need to dispute the increasingly narrowed definition of psychotherapy, each practitioner can become a local scientist. Also, Pole makes the case to encourage more dialogue and collaboration

---

237   Karon, B., & VandenBos, G. (1981). *The psychotherapy of schizophrenia: The treatment of choice.* Northvale, NJ: Jason Aronson, Inc.
238   Freedman, N., et al. (1999). Ibid.
239   Pole, N. (2000). Ibid.

between researchers and practicing clinicians. Helpfully, she would like to get away from the premise that is often posed by researchers, which pits different theoretical orientations or technical aspects of treatment approaches against one another; that is, how each compares in regard to a more discreet, often superficial "problem." Rather, Pole recommends that psychotherapists and researchers organize around what they do and how they do it in regard to a particular patient and in a particular context and that this be examined in terms of the particular impact of various practice approaches on a certain patient. Across time, data can accumulate to support more generalizable models of how to employ theories and their associated methodologies with a variety of patients and retain an element of the naturalistic qualities of real-world professional clinical practice.

It is clear that if psychoanalysis and psychoanalytical therapies are to survive in the present economical and political climate, additional research must be undertaken and more outreach across interdisciplinary lines must occur. We believe that the psychoanalytical enterprise can withstand the scrutiny of empirical investigation and more than hold its own in the marketplace of ideas.

CHAPTER 21

FINAL WORD

No theory is permanent or perfect. Psychological theories can be no more than models of the mind: they will never become one-to-one matches to a person's internal or external being, yet a good theory is subject to testing, provides useful predictions about what will work, and is open to modification. Our strong conviction is that Object-Relations Theory is just such a theory if it encompasses the insights gained from Self-Psychology and does not attempt to be one theory for all patients. Also, it must recognize and make use of the contributions of its psychoanalytic heritage (as well as other theories) where appropriate. We continue to find it useful in a wide variety of settings that continue to surprise even us, some 10 years after we first began using the theory. Students, supervisees, and colleagues report the same thing. The theory is not only robust but invariably has helpful suggestions to offer in any psychotherapy, including the difficult and blocked. In fact, some of the most interesting work in this still-developing field is in the area of negative therapeutic reactions (mentioned in a previous chapter).

Critics sometimes claim that the theory has little proof, as an earlier-cited study suggested. As one surveys the empirical backing that comes not only from psychoanalytic circles but also from developmental, experimental, and a variety of other types of research backgrounds, one sees much support and little direct challenge, unless one believes that failure to support the theory is a contradiction of the theory.[240]

We think the strongest test of the value of Object-Relations Theory comes when someone attempts to use it, as we have consistently stated. The largest obstacle to using

---

240   It is not. In fact, this is the idea of "proving the null hypothesis," and such an erroneous belief would be antithetical to scientific thinking.

the theory, as we pointed out in Chapter 1, seems to be the "impenetrable" language used to present the theory. It is hoped that this book has helped to remove that obstacle, making the theory and its use more accessible by a wider range of psychotherapists. These psychotherapists, we believe, as we stated at the outset, will then begin to hunger to read books and articles written by the experts on the finer points of Object-Relations Theory. Our hope and belief is that, having read an introduction such as the one contained in this book, the psychotherapist who is hungry for more knowledge about Self-Psychology and Object-Relations Theory will actually find him- or herself able to obtain it.

GLOSSARY

Alter ego transference

One of the several transferences typical to patients with borderline and narcissistic personalities, originally described by Kohut. The essence of the transference is that it requires another person to serve almost as a separate brain for the person to function. Unlike other primitive two-person transferences, this one contains a limited recognition of the separateness of the other person.

Alloplastic defense

One of the many names for the primitive, two-person defenses that are so symbiotic in origin that the feeling state, perception, or set of behaviors is cast on almost any external circumstance.

Autism

Sometimes discussed as a normal developmental state occurring shortly after birth but before symbiosis, whereby certain parts of the self begin organizing around the affect of pleasure and the process of association. More commonly used to describe a personality organization similar to this developmental stage with a strong, almost impenetrable defensive wall separating the person from any other person's relational energies.

Bad object

An experience from early in life whereby another person is experienced as invariably dangerous, depriving, and painful.

Bad object transference

An exceedingly difficult transference for a psychotherapist to work through, in that the psychotherapist (or another significant other) is experienced as dangerous (and quite often powerful), almost no matter what the psychotherapist may do to counterbalance the belief. To complicate matters further, the psychotherapist is strongly drawn to perform negative actions, as he or she is consistently treated in a hostile, defensive manner by the patient.

Bipolar self

A concept originated in Self-Psychology that describes the developing person's need for someone to idealize, on the one hand, while needing to be appreciatively understood, on the other.

Cathexis

A term that originated with Freud that describes loving attachment energies that one person directs toward another.

Cohesive self

A self that is centrally organized and functions in an integrated fashion as a whole.

Defenses

A concept originating with Freud that is given many more categorical types with the addition of the ways in which psychotics and personality disorders attempt to protect whatever fragile organization of the self they may have.

Deficit vs. Conflict theory

The former is a new contribution of the Object-Relations and Self-Psychology theories. It sees the possibility of simple deficits in personality structure and functioning, either through missing out on having those functions performed by caretaking objects when needed or by identification with objects whose ability to care for themselves and others is quite limited. Deficit theory implies a need for the psychotherapist either to provide nurturance for the patient in an area where that has been a missing feature in his life or see to it that such caretaking is provided.

Developmental arrest

A concept common to both older and newer forms of psychoanalytic thought, which sees psychological development stopping, with perhaps a complement of defending structures, because of trauma or lack of proper nurturance.

Dyadic

A term that refers to the personality organizations dating from early life that require the enveloping of an internal image of another person (who is not regarded as a person) to be complete, functioning, and whole.

Facilitating environment

Often misnamed the holding environment by those using today's common psychological language. The holding environment is only one subtype of the facilitating environment, which is that social environment that nurtures normal psychological development, especially during the early stages of life.

Good-enough parent

A concept coined by Winnicott, describing a caregiver who may not be perfect but is responsive enough to the developmental needs of the child for the child to progress in his or her development.

Good object

A person who is experienced not as a person, but as a process of need fulfillment and not frustration.

Handling environment

The second stage of the facilitating environment, in which the child and parent each handle physical and relational objects, enabling the child to begin to develop some sense of objectivity. The good-enough parent appreciates the child's need for this and makes sure that it happens.

Holding environment

The earliest type of facilitating environment, in which a parent holds, contains, nurtures, and protects a dependent infant.

Identification

A process whereby a person takes on personality characteristics of another through his or her psychological attachment to the other.

Incorporation

The earliest form of acquiring personality characteristics from another, whereby the characteristics become an internal operating framework in a child or person, simply acquired through felt attachment to another without the characteristics being edited or modified at all.

Internalization

The process of incorporation, identification, and introjection.

Introjection

A slightly more sophisticated process of internalization than incorporation, but similar to it, with the difference being that the personality traits are acquired more consciously.

Mirror transference

A transference requiring a great deal of empathy and appreciation on the part of the psychotherapist or object for the child or patient to have self-esteem and to function and develop properly.

Object, object-representation, and internalized object

The latter two mean essentially the same thing: the representation of the relationship to a significant other that is contained in the mind. The first term refers to the external being of the significant other.

Optimal frustration

A balance to the idea of making up deficits in patients' lives through providing therapeutic gratification; here, the patient is frustrated minimally, after having received a sufficient amount of caretaking, so that the patient identifies with the caretaking previously provided and cares for himself.

Projective identification

A defense used by persons having personality disorders whereby they tend to see noxious qualities they recognize all too well from the self in some other person who has become like a bad object to them.

Selfobject

A term (coined by Kohut) that picks up the tenor of the beliefs of almost all Object-Relations theorists and Self-Psychologists, as they see the early organization of the self requiring the presence of functions performed by what more-mature adults would recognize as another person.

Transmuting internalization

An internalization that aids in the development and fulfillment of the person by offering wise guidance.

Triadic self

A person who successfully made it to the Oedipal stage without major structural defects. Now others can be seen as distinct, rather than as poorer or better shadows of the primary caregiver. For the first time, rivalry and envy are possible.

True and false selves

These concepts originated with Winnicott, with the former representing a personality that functions out of its own feelings and need fulfillment and the latter functioning to obtain needs satisfaction indirectly through obsessive attempts to please objects.

About the University of Indianapolis Press

The University of Indianapolis Press is a nonprofit publisher of original works, specializing in, though not limited to, topics with an international orientation. It is committed to disseminating research and information in pursuit of the goals of scholarship, teaching, and service. The Press aims to foster scholarship by publishing books and monographs by learned writers for the edification of readers. It supports teaching by providing instruction and practical experience through internships and practica in various facets of publishing, including editing, proofreading, production, design, marketing, and organizational management. In the spirit of the University's motto, "Education for Service," the Press encourages a service ethic in its people and its partnerships. The University of Indianapolis Press was institutionalized in August 2003; before its institutionalization, the University of Indianapolis Press published thirteen books, eight of which were under the auspices of the Asian Programs. The Press had specialized in Asian Studies and, as part of its commitment to support projects with an international orientation, will continue to focus on this field while encouraging submission of manuscripts in other fields of study.

Books from the University of Indianapolis Press
(1992–2003)

1. Phylis Lan Lin, Winston Y. Chao, Terri L. Johnson, Joan Persell, and Alfred Tsang, eds. (1992) *Families: East and West.*
2. Wei Wou. (1993) *KMT-CCP Paradox: Guiding a Market Economy in China.*
3. John Langdon and Mary McGann. (1993) *The Natural History of Paradigms.*
4. Yu-ning Li, ed. (1994) *Images of Women in Chinese Literature.*
5. Phylis Lan Lin, Ko-Wang Mei, and Huai-chen Peng, eds. (1994) *Marriage and the Family in Chinese Societies: Selected Readings.*
6. Phylis Lan Lin and Wen-hui Tsai, eds. (1995) *Selected Readings on Marriage and the Family: A Global Perspective.*
7. Charles Guthrie, Dan Briere, and Mary Moore. (1995) *The Indianapolis Hispanic Community.*
8. Terry Kent and Marshall Bruce Gentry, eds. (1996) *The Practice and Theory of Ethics.*
9. Phylis Lan Lin and Christi Lan Lin. (1996) *Stories of Chinese Children's Hats: Symbolism and Folklore.*
10. Phylis Lan Lin and David Decker, eds. (1997) *China in Transition: Selected Essays.*
11. Phylis Lan Lin, ed. (1998) *Islam in America: Images and Challenges.*
12. Michelle Stoneburner and Billy Catchings. (1999) *The Meaning of Being Human.*
13. Frederick D. Hill. (2003) *'Downright Devotion to the Cause': A History of the University of Indianapolis and Its Legacy of Service.*

For information on the above titles or to place an order, contact:
University of Indianapolis Press
1400 East Hanna Avenue / Indianapolis, IN 46227 USA
(317) 788-3288 / (317) 788-3480 (fax)
lin@uindy.edu / http://www.uindy.edu/universitypress

University of Indianapolis Press Book List
(2004–2009)

Phylis Lan Lin and Cheng Fang. *Operational Flexibility: A Study of the Conceptualizations of Aging and Retirement in China* (in Chinese and English)	0-880938-51-X $12.95
Chiara Betta. *The Other Middle Kingdom: A Brief History of Muslims in China* (in Chinese and English). Chinese translation by Phylis Lan Lin and Cheng Fang	0-880938-53-6 $19.95
brenda Lin. *Wealth Ribbon: Taiwan Bound, America Bound*	0-880938-54-4 $16.95
Philip H. Young. *In Days of Knights: A Story for Young People*	0-880938-55-2 $16.95
James C. Hsiung. *Comprehensive Security: Challenge for Pacific Asia*	0-880938-56-0 $16.95
May-lee Chai. *Glamorous Asians: Short Stories and Essays*	0-880938-57-9 $16.95
Phylis Lan Lin, Editor. *Journey with Art Afar. Au Ho-nien Museum Catalog*, University of Indianapolis	0-880938-58-7 $35.00
Winberg Chai. *Saudi Arabia: A Modern Reader*	0-880938-59-5 $29.95
Rumen Gechev. *Sustainable Development: Economic Aspects*	0-880938-60-9 $34.95
Alyia Ma Lynn. *Muslims in China* (in Chinese and English) (Chinese translation by Phylis Lan Lin and Cheng Fang)	0-880938-61-7 $19.95
Mac Bellner & John Pomery, Editors. *Service-Learning: Intercommunity & Interdisciplinary Explorations*	0-880938-62-5 $29.95

Philip H. Young. *Sandbox World*	0-880938-63-3 $19.95
Chau Hang. *The Happy Brush: The Joy of Chinese Painting*	0-880938-64-1 $24.95
Alex Kuo. *Panda Diaries*	0-880938-65-X $16.95
Christi Lan Lin. *Symbolism of Chinese Children's Bibs: A Mother's Affectionate Embrace* (in Chinese, Japanese, and English), International Distributor	0-880938-66-8 $39.95
Kenneth Colburn & Rona Newmark, Editors. *Service-Learning Paradigms for the 21st Century: Intercommunity, Interdisciplinary & International*	0-880938-67-6 $29.95
Mel Ramaswamy, *An Immigrant Celebrates America: Reflections on America through the Fresh Eye of an Immigrant*	0-880938-68-4 $16.95
May-lee Chai, Translator. *The Autobiography of Ba Jin.*	0-880938-69-3 $16.95
Kevin Corn. *Forward Be Our Watchword: Indiana Methodism and the Modern Middle Class*	0-880938-70-9 $34.95
Mary Moore & Phylis Lan Lin, Editors. *Service-Learning in Higher Education Paradigms & Challenges*	1-880938-71-3 $44.95

For book orders, contact:
University of Indianapolis Press
lin@uindy.edu
http://www.uindy.edu/universitypress
(317) 788-3288

ABOUT THE AUTHORS

David L Downing, PsyD, received his doctorate in clinical psychology in 1985 from the Wright State University School of Professional Psychology. He is a member of the earliest generation of professionals to receive the then-revolutionary PsyD degree. Dr. Downing is presently Director of Graduate Programs in Psychology and full professor, School of Psychological Sciences, University of Indianapolis, where he teaches a variety of subjects, including psychoanalytical theories and psychotherapy. Dr. Downing is presently Dean of the Center for Psychoanalytic Study in Chicago, from which he graduated in 1994. He is the President of Section V [Psychologist-Psychoanalyst Clinicians] of the American Psychological Association Division 39 [Psychoanalysis]. He is Co-chair of the Education & Training Committee of Division 39. Dr. Downing is also past president of Section IV [Local Chapters] of Division 39 and Section Representative to the Division 39 board. He is past president and charter treasurer, as well as one of the founders of the International Federation for Psychoanalytic Education. He is past president of the Chicago Open Chapter for the Study of Psychoanalysis affiliated with Section IV [Local Chapters] of Division 39, and continues as the current treasurer as well as editor of its journal. Dr. Downing also serves on the editorial board of the journal *Psychoanalytic Psychology*.

Photo: Darlene Delbecq

Dr. Downing has more than 32 years of clinical, academic, supervisory, consultative, and organizational experience and has presided over and chaired national and international psychoanalytical organizations and conferences. He has worked to emphasize the paradigmatic diversity of contemporary psychoanalysis and psychoanalytical research and has advocated for broadening the scope of psychoanalysis to underserved, marginalized, multi-ethnic populations, and to those suffering from severe psychopathology, such as psychosis and characterological disorders. Dr. Downing has also written and presented extensively on the diverse cultural and organizational applications of psychoanalysis, including art, literature, and film. He is especially concerned with trends and the vicissitudes of the corporatization and industrialization of the mental health field—especially psychoanalysis—along with the resultant de-professionalization and proletarianization of the profession, its transmission within academia, and its impact on practitioners that is so rampant in US society.

Dr. Downing has lived and worked in Chicago for more than 21 years. He maintains a private practice in psychoanalysis, psychoanalytical psychotherapy, and consultation in Chicago and Indianapolis.

Barry Joseph Weber, MDiv, PhD, graduated from Hamilton College and studied at the University of Rochester in New York. He earned a Master of Divinity degree from Bethany Theological Seminary in Oakbrook, Illinois, and became an ordained minister and pastor. During the Viet Nam War era he became a conscientious objector and counselled others who opposed the war. He went on to earn his doctorate in clinical psychology from Loyola University in Chicago and founded his own group psychological practice in the northwest suburbs of Chicago. Before it was more commonly accepted, he championed the inclusion of psychologists in divorce mediation and child custody hearings—something that is almost a given today. Through his efforts, Dr. Weber also helped design the nature of training and education leading to professionals' qualification/certification for effective practice in these arenas. After becoming a certified forensic psychologist, he wrote two books. He then became an adjunct instructor of psychology at several university programs in the Chicago area, including the Illinois School of Professional Psychology, and was a supervisor for doctoral- and master's-level professionals-in-training in his group private practice, which he also developed into a training program for professional psychologists. Among Dr. Weber's passions were extending psychoanalytical thought and practice into novel domains and transmitting this uniquely healing process to successive generations of clinicians. He died unexpectedly in 2002 of a heart attack at the age of 54.

INDEX OF AUTHORS, SCIENTISTS, ARTISTS, AND OTHER PEOPLE REFERENCED

Notes:
- Page numbers followed by n refer to a footnote as numbered.
- Subjects and topics are listed in the Subject Index, immediately following this index.

SUBJECT INDEX

Notes:

* Page numbers followed by f or t refer to figures or tables, respectively.
* People are listed in the Index of Authors, Scientists, Artists, and Other People Referenced, immediately preceding this Subject Index.

behavioristic theory, 148–149, 158
Bell South, 143n202
Berkeley Psychotherapy Research Project,
   158
biological approach to mental disturbance, 26, 64–65
Bipolar Personality Disorders:
   compared to rapprochement child, 95,
      97, 98, 100n129
   counter-transference reactions, 78
   and DSM-IV-TR diagnosis, 67
   origin of, 63
bipolar self, 164
birth, 45, 154
Borderline Personality Disorder, 71–82
   adolescents diagnosed as, 122
   Antisocial Personality Disorder as, 106
   characteristics of, 72–73, 82
   compared to rapprochement child,
      100n129, 101
   counter-transference reactions, 78–82
   nature of problems, 75–78
   origins in developmental stage, 63,
      74–75
   paranoid personality as, 108
   therapeutic techniques, 78–82
   treatment of, 75–78
Boulder, Colorado conference, 17
boundaries:
   Borderline Personality Disorder and, 78
   in infant development, 47, 60
   paranoid personality and, 109
British Object Relations School, 55–58, 74

C
case analyses of patients, 147–148
case managers in MCOs, 144–145
catharsis, 42
cathexis, 32, 164
causality, principle of, 30
Change (Watzlawick, Weakland, and
   Fisch), 126
child abuse, 30, 106
children, 50–54, 55, 154–155
   See also developmental theory; in-
      fants.
classical psychoanalysis:
   choosing the correct therapeutic ap-
      proach, 139

comparisons to other theories, 27,
   43–44, 55, 56, 57
free association in, 43
fundamental rule of, 37–38
cognitive-behavioristic approach, 26, 140,
   148–149, 158
cognitive psychotherapy, 120
cohesive self, 164
The Collected Papers on Schizophrenia
   (Searles), 131
college students, 121–122
Columbia Medical Plan, 143n202
communication in psychotherapy, 37–38
conflict, as curative technique, 79–80
conflict theory, 164
conflicted internalizations, 137
conflicts in developmental stages,
   112–114, 117–118
confusion, 126
conscious, in psychoanalytical theory, 29
consciousness, 24
   stream of, 46
conservation of energy, 33
couch, 28, 40, 44
counter-transference reactions:
   to Antisocial Personality Disorder,
      108, 110
   to Borderline Personality Disorder,
      78–82
   to Narcissistic Personality Disorder,
      88–90
   to rapprochement child, 99–101, 103
   to rebellious teenager by Freud, 148
   to schizophrenia, 62–65
   understanding for therapeutic im-
      passe, 129, 130–133
crises, life, 125–128, 140
cultural phenomena, and Freud, 156

D
deanimated frozen wall, 61, 62, 63, 75
death drive (thanatos), 19
defense mechanisms, 150
defenses, 164
deficient behavior, 57–58
deficit theory, 102, 164
deficits:
   in Borderline Personality Disorder,
      77–78, 80

fragmenting self, 84n95
free association, 37–38, 43, 139–140
frequency of therapy, 28, 159
Freudian psychoanalysis. *See* classical
   psychoanalysis.
friendships, forming, 155
frustrating object. *See* bad object.

G
genetic point of view, 30, 38
good-enough parent, 165
good object:
   in Borderline Personality Disorder,
      76–77
   defined, 48–53, 165
   in Narcissistic Personality Disorder, 86
   and rapprochement, 94–97
grandiosity:
   of Antisocial Personality Disorder, 107
   of Narcissistic Personality Disorder,
      63, 91–92
   of rapprochement child, 97, 99
gratifying object. *See* good object.
grief, 125, 126
group psychotherapy, 120

H
hallucination, 60–61, 65
handling environment, 165
hatching (stage 4):
   in Borderline Personality Disorder,
      74–75
   in developmental theory, 49–50, 53
   individuation in, 50, 51–52, 85, 93
   in rapprochement child, 93–94
health insurance, 143n202, 144
health maintainance organizations:
   managed care organizations (MCOs),
      144–145
hebephrenic schizophrenia, 60
Helmholt's principle, 33
holding environment, 165, 166
hospitalizations, 81–82, 145
human development. *See* development,
   human.
hydraulics, 18, 33
hyperindividualism, 63, 85
hypomanic patient, 102
hysteria, 42, 147–148

I
id, in Freud's tripartite model, 19, 30–32,
   36, 136
idealizing transference, 88, 90–91, 107
identification:
   with the aggressor, 35
   ego as body of, 31
   as process in internalization, 136, 166
   projective, 90, 136, 167
identity disorders, 120
incorporation, 135, 166
independence, in Borderline Personality
   Disorder, 75–76
Independent Object Relations (British)
   School, 56, 57, 74
individuality, 63, 85, 155
individuation in hatching stage, 50,
   51–52, 85, 93
infants, 45–49, 150–152, 154
   See also children; developmental
      theory.
inpatient treatment, 145
insight, 37, 40, 42–44
Institute for Psychoanalysis in Chicago, 55
Interferon, 125
internal working models (IWMs), 152
internalizations, 135–138, 166
internalized mother, 157
internalized object, 166
interpretations, in treatment, 39, 40, 43
introjection, 135, 166

L
lability of affect, 61
lacunae, 38
latency period psychopathologies, 117–120
learning, and unconscious, 150
libido, 32
life crises, 125–128, 140
life transitions, 37
listening, 38, 127, 128
long-term psychotherapy, 143–145,
   158–159

M
malignant narcissist personality, 108
managed care organizations (MCOs),
   144–145
management and containment, 140